Batsford's Walking Guides: South Downs

Batsford's Walking Guides: South Downs

*Written and compiled
by Jilly MacLeod*

BATSFORD

First published in the United Kingdom in 2011 by
Batsford
10 Southcombe Street
London
W14 0RA
An imprint of Anova Books Company Ltd

Materials kindly provided by individual organizations,
as credited at the end of each walk.

Walks on pages 12 and 24 © Natural England 2011.
Material is reproduced with the permission of Natural
England, http://www.naturalengland.org.uk/copyright

ISBN 9781906388867

A CIP catalogue for this book is available from
the British Library.

20 19 18 17 16 15 14 13 12 11
10 9 8 7 6 5 4 3 2 1

Reproduction by Rival Colour Ltd, UK
Printed by 1010 Printing International Ltd, China

This book can be ordered direct from the publisher
at the website www.anovabooks.com, or try your
local bookshop.

Neither the publisher nor the author can accept
responsibility for any changes, errors or omissions
in this guide, or for any loss or injury incurred
during any of the walks.

Contents

Map of the South Downs

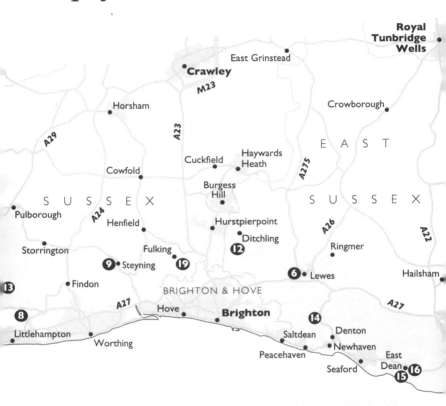

KEY TO MAP

1) Three Ways Walk
2) Walberton Woodland Walk
3) Rivers and Ruins
4) East Hampshire Hike
5) In Gilbert White's Footsteps
6) Destination Blackcap
7) Fields, Copses and Hangers
8) Park and Woodland Walk
9) Chanctonbury Ring Hill Fort
10) Duncton and Woolavington Downs
11) Poets, Parks and Waterfalls
12) Ditchling Beacon to Devil's Dyke
13) Burpham Down Circuit
14) Round Tower Ramble
15) The Seven Sisters
16) Heritage Coastline Walk
17) The Drovers Circuit
18) Black Down Woodland Walk
19) Ancient Tracks and Forts
20) Harting Down Wildlife Walk

Introduction

The South Downs form a uniquely beautiful and tranquil part of the British Isles: only an hour's drive from London, yet they provide some remarkably remote destinations for walkers in search of the great outdoors, with wide open spaces, big skies and spectacular views. Designated a National Park in 2010, the downs comprise a chalk ridge running 160km (100 miles) east to west, from Eastbourne in East Sussex, through West Sussex and on into Hampshire, terminating at Winchester. The eastern region provides some classic downland scenery with dry rolling hills cut through with rivers flowing from the Weald to the sea. West Sussex is more heavily wooded, while the Hampshire Downs are lower and dominated by farmland, pasture and parkland. The whole area was originally heavily wooded, but widespread tree clearance in the Iron Age and subsequent sheep grazing created large areas of chalk grassland, much of which was ploughed up following World War II. Chalk grassland is now one of Britain's most threatened habitats and conservation bodies, such as the National Trust, are reintroducing grazing to help restore parts of the landscape to its original form.

The rocks that make up the South Downs were formed beneath the sea about 120 million years ago. Movements in the earth's crust uplifted these rocks to create a vast dome which was subsequently worn away by rivers and the elements to form the landscape we see today. The northern edge of the eastern downs comprises a steep, often wooded escarpment that rises dramatically above the Weald (an area of lowland between the North and South Downs, part of which also sits within the National Park). To the south the landscape falls away more gently in a broad rolling dip-slope that meets the sea at the precipitous cliffs of the Seven Sisters and Beachy Head. This eastern area is perhaps best described by Rudyard Kipling who referred to the 'blunt, bow-headed, whale-backed downs'.

Visitors to the South Downs, of which there are 100 million every year, are rewarded with over 2,000 miles of well-marked footpaths and trails, including the 160km (100 mile) South Downs Way, which largely follows drove roads and other ancient routes – some dating back 6,000 years – along the crest of the chalk downland ridge. Distinctive features to look out for include Bronze Age barrows (burial mounds), Iron Age hill forts, sculpted dry valleys, or coombes, and man-made dew ponds, created to provide livestock with water on the otherwise dry uplands.

THE WALKS

The walks featured in this book cover a wide range of different landscapes and points of interest: many follow the South Downs Way across rolling downlands (pages 12, 44, 48, 56) and coastal cliff tops (pages 68 and 72), affording spectacular views in all directions; others pass along quiet river valleys (pages 20, 32 and 64) or through ancient woods (pages 24 and 36) and hangers (page 28), nature reserves (pages 76) and historic parkland (pages 40 and 52). Wildlife features widely, with walks across some of Britain's most precious habitats: limestone grassland (pages 84 and 88) and heathland (pages 52 and 80), with their associated wild flowers and insects; and beech woodland carpeted with bluebells in spring (page 76). Then there are the special-interest walks: seeking out ancient hill forts (page 44 and 84), Roman villas (page 52), battle sites (page 12), medieval churches (page 64) and windmills (page 56); or following in the footsteps of famous people, such as 18th-century naturalist Gilbert White (page 28) and authors Mervyn Peak (page 60) and Virginia Woolf (page 64).

Nearly all the walks are circular, many with traditional country pubs along the way where you can stop off for some welcome refreshments. General advice on how to reach your starting point is provided, and although some areas are relatively remote it is always good to consider whether you can leave the car at home and take public transport (check online at www.traveline.org.uk before you go, or find out about the 'Breeze up to the Downs' bus service from Brighton at www.brighton-hove.gov.uk). Also provided are suggestions for local attractions that you may wish to combine with your walk, such as nearby gardens, castles, country-house estates, wildlife parks and museums.

WALKING THE SOUTH DOWNS

- Many of the walks may be damp and muddy after rain, so always wear suitable footwear: walking shoes or boots are advisable.
- If you are walking alone, let someone know where you are and when you expect to return.
- Consider taking a mobile phone with you, bearing in mind coverage can be patchy in rural areas.
- It is always advisable to take an Ordnance Survey map with you on country walks, to supplement the maps provided.

- Some of the walks take you along small country lanes without pavements. Always walk facing oncoming traffic (except when approaching a right-hand bend when it is advisable to cross the road for a clear view), keep children and dogs under close control, and wear something light or brightly coloured when visibility is poor (e.g. at dusk).
- Take special care of children when walking beside water or along cliff tops.
- Support the rural economy by spending your money in the local facilities, such as shops, cafés and pubs.
- While the author has taken every care to ensure the accuracy of this guidebook, changes to the walking routes may occur after publication.
- Public transport may also change over time, so if you are thinking of taking a bus to your destination, always check timetables and routes online or with local tourist information centres before setting out.

FOLLOW THE COUNTRYSIDE CODE

Here's how to respect, protect and enjoy the countryside:

- Always park sensibly, making sure that your vehicle is not blocking access to drives, fields and farm tracks.
- Leave gates as you find them or follow instructions on signs. If walking in a group, make sure the last person knows how to leave a gate.
- In fields where crops are growing, follow the paths wherever possible.
- Use gates, stiles or gaps in field boundaries when provided – climbing over walls, hedges and fences causes damage.
- Don't leave litter and leftover food – it not only spoils the beauty of the countryside but can be dangerous to wildlife and farm animals as well.
- Keep all dogs under strict control, particularly near livestock, and observe any requests to keep dogs on leads. (Remember, by law farmers are entitled to destroy a dog that injures or worries their animals.)
- Always clean up after your dog and get rid of the mess responsibly.
- Take special care not to damage, destroy or remove flowers, trees or even rocks: they provide homes and food for wildlife, and add to everybody's enjoyment of the countryside.
- Don't get too close to wild animals and farm animals as they can behave unpredictably.
- Be careful not to disturb ruins and historic sites.
- Be careful not to drop a match or smouldering cigarette at any time of the year, as this can cause fires.
- Get to know the signs and symbols used in the countryside. Visit the 'Finding your way' pages on Natural England's website for more information*.

* For full details of the countryside code, visit
www.naturalengland.org.uk/ourwork/enjoying/countrysidecode/

11

Three Ways Walk

CHERITON, HINTON AMPNER AND KILMESTON

This pleasant, easy walk across the undulating Hampshire countryside takes you through fields and woodland, alongside hedgerows and past historic buildings, crossing 18 stiles along the way. Setting out from the village of Cheriton, it connects three walking routes – the Wayfarer's Walk, the Itchen Way and the South Downs Way – and provides a number of stunning viewpoints across the downs. En route you pass the site of the Battle of Cheriton (1644) and the glorious 20th-century gardens at Hinton Ampner, following which you have the opportunity to stop off at The Milbury's, a 17th-century freehouse in a converted mill, listed among the strangest pubs in Britain.

DISTANCE:	16km (10 miles) (circular)
TIME:	Allow 4½ – 6 hours
LEVEL:	Easy (but with 18 stiles)
START/PARKING:	Cheriton village green, with on-street parking (SO24 0PX). OS grid reference SU582285 (OS Explorer map 132)
GETTING THERE:	*By car:* Turn off A31 between Alton and Winchester on to B3046 to Cheriton
	By public transport: Train to Petersfield Station, then take bus no. 67 towards Winchester
REFRESHMENTS:	Flower Pots Inn, Cheriton, or The Milbury's (en route)
LOCAL ATTRACTIONS:	Hinton Ampner House and Gardens (National Trust)

DIRECTIONS

1. From the main road on the village green, head down the track signposted to the church and after a few metres take the footpath off to the right, signed Wayfarer's Walk (but also part of the Itchen Way). Follow this path diagonally across the field to a lane, beside some farm buildings.

2. Cross the lane and continue along the path opposite, passing through the grassy fields, with the hedgerow on your right, towards a stile. The River

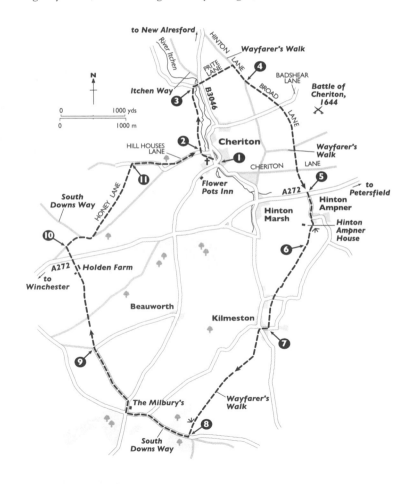

Itchen runs to your right here but is obscured by the hedgerow. Cross the stile, and carry on over two more stiles in the fence lines. Continue past some houses and on to a lane that takes you through a yard, past some weeping willow trees, and on to a road.

3. Turn right here, following the sign for the Itchen Way over the river, with its wild watercress beds, and on to the main road heading north out of Cheriton, where the Itchen Way peels off to the left. Cross the road with care and carry on straight ahead along the track (Prite Lane), following the Wayfarer's Walk gently uphill until you reach a T-junction. Turn right (on to Hinton Lane) and follow the track for about 500m (550yd) until you reach a fork.

4. Bear left (on to Broad Lane) and continue along the track to the junction with Badshear Lane (a metalled road), where you cross straight over, heading towards Hinton Ampner. From here you get good views to your left across the site of the Battle of Cheriton, where the Parliamentarians won a decisive victory over Royalist forces on 29th March 1644 during the English Civil War. Shortly you rejoin the Wayfarer's Walk, which merges from the right. Continue straight ahead between the hedgerows, crossing Cheriton Lane and passing Primrose Cottages to reach the A272.

5. Cross the road with care and continue straight ahead, following the lane up a short hill, with Hinton Ampner Estate on your right. Continue through the iron gates and shortly after leave the roadway through a kissing gate signed Wayfarer's Walk. Keep to the right-hand path at the fork, skirting round Hinton Ampner gardens and gaining a good view over the countryside to the south. Continue on through a gate and a further kissing gate to reach a large grassed field.

6. Follow the path across the field, crossing the stile beside the field gate, then cross another field to a stile. Continue across a further field, with a bank and trees to the right, to a stile that takes you on to a lane. Turn right up the lane for a very short distance, then immediately left

at a fingerpost, crossing over the single-step stile. Cross the fields, following the line of telegraph poles, and continue through the woodland, passing through a pair of gates and on to a lane.

7. Follow the fingerpost to the right along the lane, passing a green and crossing the road at Kilmeston with care, to join the path at a fingerpost and two-step stile. Cross a small field with a row of poplars to the left, exiting over a single-step stile. Follow the path over two planks spanning the ditch and two stiles, with a wooded strip on your right. Carry on through the gap in the hedge beside a fingerpost and cross two large fields to a two-step stile in the corner. Go up the grassy slope and on over a stile, from where there is a good view back to the north.

8. Shortly, the path joins the road beside a fingerpost. Turn right here to follow the South Downs Way, which runs through a wooded strip before rejoining the road after 0.8km (½ mile). Continue along the road to the crossroads, where refreshments can be had in The Milbury's pub. Turn right and after a short distance turn left at the fingerpost to follow the South Downs Way along the lane.

9. After nearly 1km (⅔ mile), where the surfaced road bends to the right, continue straight ahead along the track to join the A272 just beyond Holden Farm. Cross the road with care and follow the fingerpost up a moderate slope on a gravelled track until you reach a T-junction with a fingerpost.

10. Turn right here, following the field edge to a gate in the corner, where the South Downs Way peels off to the left. Continue ahead through the gate and into a wooded strip. At the junction, bear left up Honey Lane (marked as a restricted byway) and follow the track for nearly 1.5km (1 mile) to a junction beside a large barn.

11. Turn right and follow the hard-topped road to a junction, where the road bends to the right. Continue straight ahead here, sloping down through the woods with banks on both sides until you reach Hill Houses Lane, which takes you back into Cheriton.

Courtesy of Natural England/South Downs Way National Trail. For more information and similar walks see www.nationaltrail.co.uk/southdowns

Walberton Woodland Walk

WALBERTON AND ARUNDEL

*This attractive walk takes you from the West Sussex
town of Walberton through fields and woodlands to historic
Arundel, with its Norman castle dramatically perched on
the hilltop, cobbled streets and medieval buildings. From here
you climb steeply uphill and return through Rewell Wood,
a broad-leaved woodland that is carefully managed by the
Forestry Commission in order to encourage butterflies, such as the
increasingly threatened pearl-bordered fritillary, and rare moths
including the scarce merveille du jour, the clay fan-foot and
the waved carpet moth. For a shorter walk, you can follow
the upland route from Arundel to Walberton, then return
by bus to your starting point.*

DISTANCE:	13.5km (8½ miles) (circular) or 9km (5½ miles) linear (returning by bus to Arundel)
TIME:	Allow 4–5 hours (shorter route: 2½–3½ hours
LEVEL:	Moderate (with a long steady climb)
START/PARKING:	Car park at Walberton Village Hall (BN18 0PH). OS grid reference SU972059 (OS Explorer map 121). Park in Arundel for linear walk
GETTING THERE:	*By car:* Turn off A27, about 11km (7 miles) east of Chichester, on to Yapton Lane, turning right on to The Street in Walberton *By public transport:* Train to Arundel, then take bus no. 84 towards Chichester, or train to Barnham Station, then take bus no. 66 towards Bognor Regis, alighting in Walberton
REFRESHMENTS:	The Holly Tree, Walberton
LOCAL ATTRACTIONS:	Arundel Castle

DIRECTIONS

1. From the car park turn left along The Street to Yapton Lane. Cross the lane, go through the kissing gate and along the path past the lone tree in the field to the kissing gate at the edge of the golf course. Continue down the gravelled path and across the bridge over Binsted Rife to the end of the gravel. Turn half right and walk straight up the hill and alongside the Binsted churchyard wall to the kissing gate leading into Binsted Lane West.

2. Cross the lane and follow the often muddy path by the side of the Old Rectory wall. Where the hedges end, continue straight on across the field and through Spinning Wheel Copse, where there is usually a brilliant show of bluebells to the north in the spring. Follow the path to the left and then bear right round the edge of the next field to enter Binsted Woods. Continue downhill to a wooden bridge across a ditch and on to Binsted Lane East.

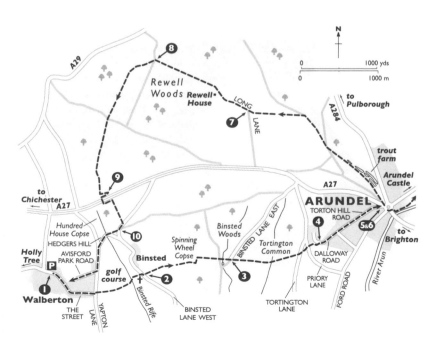

3. Cross the lane and veer slightly left to cross into Tortington Common, a woodland area that usually has muddy patches. Continue along the path, crossing a wooden bridge over a stream and climbing gently through a Scots pine plantation to reach Tortington Lane. Cross the lane and follow the path through the paddock to Priory Lane.

Cross the lane, go over the stile opposite and continue through these woods to another stile leading on to Dalloway Road in Arundel.

4. Turn half right down Dalloway Road and follow it round to the left and into Torton Hill Road (from where you get a fine view of Arundel Castle). Carry on down to the grassy area beside the roundabout where Ford Road meets the A27.

5. From here you can either head back to Walberton or carry on and explore Arundel. To head back go straight to direction 6 below. Otherwise, bear slightly right across the grass and cross Ford Road with care to the path that leads down by the side of the bridge over the River Arun. Bear left under the bridge to a path running between new houses, following it to a bend in the road. Bear right and continue right down Tarrant Street to the High Street, making your way back to the grassy area beside the roundabout (point 5/6 on the map) when you are ready.

6. Cross the A27 with care and turn into the tarmac lane between the twin lodges. Follow the lane for about 0.8km (½ mile) and just past the entrance to the trout farm bear left to follow the path uphill. At the top of the hill bear right along a farm track, ignoring the path that goes downhill to the right. At the 'Private' sign, turn left through a farm gate and follow the bridleway half right across a field to another iron gate. Continue along this bridleway until you reach Long Lane coming in from the left, leading to Rewell House.

7. Carry on straight ahead for about 0.4km (¼ mile) to the edge of a copse, where the path leaves Long Lane and goes off to the right around the grounds of the house and past a gate into Rewell Woods. Continue along the path for about 0.8km (½ mile) as it follows a logging track, carrying on straight ahead at the crossing of the tracks until you reach the point where the logging track turns sharp left and the bridleway goes straight on through a narrow wood.

8. Ignoring both these routes, take the path that goes half left into the woods: in summer the foxgloves provide a brilliant display here. Follow this track for about 1km (²/₃ mile) to the 'Clapham Junction' of Rewell Woods where a number of tracks meet. Take the one that goes slightly left between two large beech trees, following it between a Corsican-pine plantation on the left and a sweet-chestnut coppice on the right. It later follows a ridge between an old quarry and a valley and then a wooden post-and-rail fence on the left. Continue down a steepish bank and turn sharp left to where the old A27 comes in from the right.

9. Double back down this and cross a steel motorcycle barrier to get to the side of the new A27. Taking good care, cross straight over the road and go through the gate into Hundred House Copse. Turn left by the side of a wooden fence bounding the road and continue to another wide gate where the path turns right. Follow the path, avoiding the archery-practice land, and cross a field to Binsted Lane West. Bear right down the lane for some 100m (110yd) to a stile on the right.

10. Cross the stile and follow the path to Hedgers Hill, where you turn right. Continue to Yapton Lane, bear left and then turn right into Avisford Park Road, at the end of which the ensuing footpath takes you back to the village hall car park.

Courtesy of Walberton Action Group. For more information and similar walks go to www.walbertonag.org.uk

Rivers and Ruins

Midhurst and Easebourne

The route begins in the historic town of Midhurst, once home to the author HG Wells and the site of a Norman castle. From here you head north to explore the surrounding countryside, following the River Rother through National Trust land before branching off across the fields, over stiles and through a chestnut coppice to reach the attractive village of Easebourne, where The White Swan public house offers welcome refreshments. The way then takes you past the beautiful Easebourne Priory and on to Cowdray ruins, a Tudor mansion recently saved from total collapse by the Cowdray Heritage Trust. From here you have the option of visiting the remains of Midhurst Castle before returning to your starting point.

DISTANCE:	13km (8 miles) (circular)
TIME:	Allow 4–5 hours
LEVEL:	Moderate (with some fairly steep slopes)
START/PARKING:	Angel Hotel, North Street, Midhurst (GU29 9DN). Park in North Street car park. OS grid reference SU886217 (OS Explorer map 120)
GETTING THERE:	*By car:* About 21km (13 miles) south of Haslemere, on A286 Haslemere/Chichester road, or east of Petersfield on A272
	By public transport: Train to Haslemere Station, then bus no. 70 to Midhurst (not Sundays)
REFRESHMENTS:	The White Horse, Easebourne, or a wide choice of pubs and cafés in Midhurst
LOCAL ATTRACTIONS:	Cowdray ruins; Woolbeding Garden (National Trust)

DIRECTIONS

1. The walk starts at The Angel Hotel, which dates back to the 15th century. During the 1880s HG Wells took rooms in a house beside The Angel and some of his early novels are based around Midhurst. With your back to the hotel, walk to your left up North Street and turn right down June Lane, crossing the road with care. Continue down June Lane to The Half Moon pub on the left, at the junction with the main road. Bear sharp right here, taking the footpath towards Woolbeding.

COWDRAY RUINS

Originally owned by the Viscounts Montague and dating back to the early 1500s, Cowdray was, in its heyday, a fine Tudor mansion, visited by both Henry VIII and Elizabeth I. But a devastating fire on 24th September 1793 saw it reduced to a ruin, after which the remaining fabric simply rotted away, visited only by writers, scholars and artists such as William Turner and John Constable. Minor restoration work undertaken in the early years of the 20th century helped to save the building from total collapse, but it was nonetheless added to English Heritage's 'At Risk' register. The building is now in the care of the Cowdray Heritage Trust who recently undertook a massive two-year restoration and stabilization project, completed in 2007, which breathed welcome life back into this significant relic of the Tudor Age.

2. Following the field edge, go through two kissing gates and, at the third one, bear left and follow the track to the road. Turn right here and go over Woolbeding Bridge, which dates back to the early medieval period.

3. Continue along the road and where it bends sharp right take the National Trust footpath on the left, heading towards the river. Follow this permissive path along the River Rother until you join a footpath. Bear left here and continue along the path, crossing over the stile and the bridges. As you follow the river, look out for pink purslane and river water crowfoot during the spring.

4. Cross the stile opposite Stedham Mill and turn right up the hill to the road. Turn right here, and then take the next footpath on the left, following the edge of the fields. At the next stile turn right and continue along the path to the road.

5. Cross the road with care on to the footpath opposite. At the next junction turn right and follow the fence round. When you reach the next junction turn right (path not marked as a public right of way) and go down past Eastshaw Farm.

6. Turn left on to the next footpath, going up the steps and over the stile. Cross two fields

and head into the chestnut coppice, following the path through the woods. Take the right-hand footpath at the next junction and then turn right down the lane towards Lock's Cottage.

7. Take the next footpath on the left and go up the steps, over the stile and into a field. Follow the footpath, crossing three stiles before you reach the road by Whitters Farm. Cross the road and go up the steps and over a stile, then follow the path through the field and downhill to another stile that takes you on to a lane. Follow the lane down to the A286, turn right and walk carefully along the road.

8. Take the next path on the left which doubles back parallel to the road. Turn right at the footpath and up some steps, then follow the field edge until you reach a T-junction. Turn right here and follow the footpath to the next waymark. Turn left, then go right through the hedge and turn left by the allotments. At the cemetery turn right and carry on down the lane into Easebourne village. At the junction turn left towards the main road and continue following the pavement round to the left. If you are in need of refreshments, a short detour to the left down Easebourne Street takes you to The White Horse public house. Back on the main road, cross the road with care and continue down past the church on your right.

9. Take the next turning on the right, following the footpath sign past Easebourne Priory, founded in 1210 by the Augustinian nuns. Follow the track down to Cowdray ruins: Cowdray was burnt out in 1793 but even as a ruin it is an impressive monument to Tudor architecture (see special feature, opposite). Opposite the ruins, turn right and follow the footpath back to the car park or the bus stop beside the tourist information office. Alternatively, you can make a short detour at this point, following the footpath round to the left to St Anne's Hill, where the remains of a Norman castle can be found.

Courtesy of the South Downs Joint Committee and the South Downs
National Park Authority. For more information go to www.southdowns.gov.uk

East Hampshire Hike

EAST MEON, MERCURY PARK AND DRAYTON

*Your walk starts in the picturesque village of East Meon,
which lies nestled in the famous Meon Valley in East Hampshire.
Affording magnificent views along the way, the route takes you
through fields, paddocks and ancient woodland, over stiles and
across open downs, following the South Downs Way for nearly half
its length and providing the option of a shortcut for those with less
time to spare. The longer route gives you the opportunity to visit
the Sustainability Centre (a working example of sustainability
that aims to inspire people to make positive changes to the way
they live and work) where you can stop for refreshments.*

DISTANCE:	13km (8 miles) (circular) with shorter route of 8km (5 miles)
TIME:	Allow 4–5 hours (shorter route: 2½–3½ hours)
LEVEL:	Moderate (with a steep ascent and descent)
START/PARKING:	East Meon High Street, by the village stores (GU32 1NW), parking in car park on Workhouse Lane. OS grid reference SU6795221 (OS Explorer map 132)
GETTING THERE:	*By car:* Turn off A3 at Petersfield on to A272, turning left at Langrish on to The Hyde which takes you into East Meon *By public transport:* Train to Petersfield Station then take bus no. 67 towards Winchester
REFRESHMENTS:	Ye Olde George Inn, East Meon, or The Beech Café at the Sustainability Centre
LOCAL ATTRACTIONS:	Buster Ancient Farm

DIRECTIONS

1. From the village stores follow the signs towards the school. Turn left into Chapel Street, past the school and round to the right on to Coombe Road. At the far end of the residential parking area on your left, follow the footpath sign through the gate and along the edge of the field.

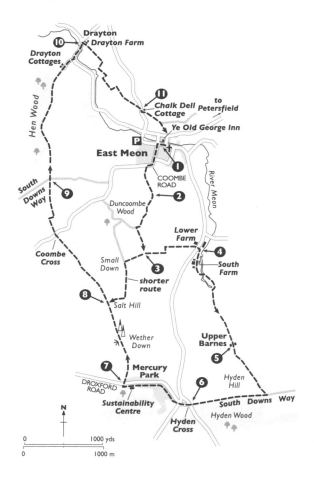

2. At the end of the straight hedge line follow the footpath sign across the field to the opposite corner. Continue along the footpath on the left field edge towards the woodland, where you cross a stile and follow the path sharp right uphill through the edge of Duncoombe Wood. At the top of the short slope go through the field gate and continue along the footpath, leading away from the woods and keeping the hedgerow on your left.

3. Upon reaching the next field gate you have a choice. For the shorter route, turn right here and head up the steep slope to the top of Small Down. At the top, turn left at the T-junction of footpaths and follow the path until you rejoin the main route at point 8 on the map (go straight to direction 8, below). For the longer route, go through the gate and turn left, following the path along the field edges (keeping them on your left). As you approach Lower Farm you come to a gap in the hedge in front of you – go through this and turning left you will see the distinctive 13th-century spire of All Saints' Church, East Meon. Now turn right and follow the hedge line to the road.

4. Cross the road and go over the stile opposite into a small paddock. Cross the paddock to the opposite corner and go through the gate into South Farm. Being careful of farm machinery, follow the main concrete track through the farm to the bridge over the small stream, which runs from the source of the River Meon. Cross the bridge and follow the path towards Upper Barnes, passing through an avenue of mature beech trees: look out for a carved wooden statue of an owl under the first tree on your left.

5. At Upper Barnes follow the footpath though the field gates, bearing left along the path to climb up the side of Hyden Hill. Upon reaching the top of the hill go over the stile to meet the South Downs Way, where you turn right. The route now follows the South Downs Way for roughly the next 4.5km (3 miles). Follow the path through the edges of Hyden Wood – an ancient woodland site that includes hazel coppice, mature beech and some conifer plantation.

6. At Hyden Cross follow the waymarked route along the road for about 150m (165yd) until you reach a small lay-by on your left where the South Downs Way leaves the road. Follow this route past the Sustainability Centre on your left (where you can stop for refreshments at the Beech Café, Thursday–Sunday) and the HMS Mercury on your right (now redundant, but once an important naval communications training facility).

7. Cross over Droxford Road and turn right, following the South Downs Way northwards towards Wether Down. As you approach the barns and the aerials at the top, look behind you to be rewarded with magnificent views across the downs and the coastal plain of Hampshire to the Isle of Wight. Carry on past the aerials and over Salt Hill until you meet a path off to the right – this is where the shorter route joins up with the longer one.

8. If you took the shorter route, cross the stile and turn right on to the South Downs Way. Otherwise, continue straight on. At Coombe Cross, cross the road and follow the wooded lane opposite for about 0.8km (½ mile) until you reach a junction where the South Downs Way heads off to the left.

9. Continue straight on here along the public byway signposted to East Meon. Follow the route through the edge of Hen Wood towards Drayton and continue along the lane on the far side of the wood past Drayton Cottages. At the forked junction bear left and follow the road next to the small River Meon. Just before the first paddock on your right at Drayton Farm take the footpath between the field fence and the hedge, crossing the stile at the top.

10. Go though the field gate directly in front of you and follow the path as it twists and turns along the field edges, keeping the edges on your right for the first two fields and on your left for the second two, and passing through gates and crossing stiles along the way until you reach a road.

11. Turn right past Chalk Dell Cottage. At the second entrance to the gravel driveway turn left, following the small footpath sign, and then immediately right. Follow the path over the stiles and across the fields as you head downhill towards East Meon church. Cross the road with care and walk down Church Street, turning right at the T-junction to take you back to your starting point.

Courtesy of Natural England/South Downs Way National Trail. For more information and similar walks see www.nationaltrail.co.uk/southdowns

In Gilbert White's Footsteps

SELBORNE AND EMPSHOTT

*Setting out from the attractive village of Selborne, home
to the famous 18th-century literary naturalist Gilbert White
(see special feature, page 31), this walk enables you to explore the
glorious landscape of the East Hampshire Hangers (steeply wooded
hillsides). Your route takes you through nature reserves, fields and
hangers, past rivers and lakes, over stiles and along country lanes,
briefly joining up with the Hangers Way. It includes some steep
slopes characteristic of the chalk and greensand hangers, and the
spring flowers and autumn colours are especially rewarding.
Gilbert's home, The Wakes, is open to the public and also
houses the Oates Collection – both are well worth a visit.*

DISTANCE:	13km (8 miles) (circular)
TIME:	Allow 4–5 hours
LEVEL:	Moderate (with some steep slopes)
START/PARKING:	In front of The Selborne Arms (GU34 3JR). Park in Selborne car park. OS grid reference SU742336 (OS Explorer map 133)
GETTING THERE:	*By car:* Turn off A3 between Liphook and Petersfield, or A31 between Farnham and Winchester, on to B3006 to Selborne
	By public transport: Train to Alton Station, then take bus no. 38 towards Petersfield, alighting at The Selborne Arms
REFRESHMENTS:	The Selborne Arms and a tea room in Selborne
LOCAL ATTRACTIONS:	Gilbert White's House and Garden; Jane Austen's House Museum, Chawton

DIRECTIONS

1. With your back to the pub, turn right along the B3006 until you see the Lion's Mouth horse trough and fountain, presented to the village in memory of Gilbert White. Take the footpath on the right-hand side, alongside the stream, and follow the path towards Noar Hill Nature Reserve, which is managed by the Hampshire Wildlife Trust. The beech woodlands were badly damaged during the gales of 1987. However, the site remains important for

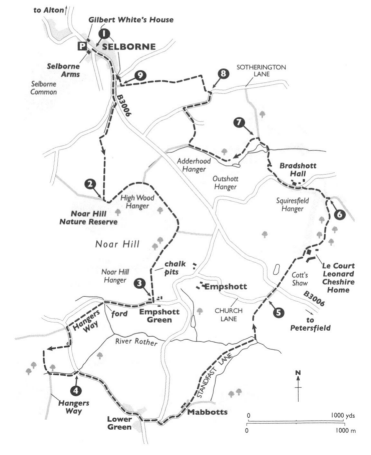

a number of orchid, butterfly and grasshopper species –
in particular, the brown hairstreak and Duke of
Burgundy butterflies.

2. Where you meet the bridleway at the base of the hanger,
   turn left and follow the lower track round the bottom of Noar
   Hill for about 0.5km (¹/₃ mile). About 100m (110yd) past the old chalk pits
   on the left-hand side, take the bridleway to the left and immediately turn
   right on to a footpath that follows the field edge before turning left across
   some fields. At the far side of the fields cross some stiles on to a lane.

3. Turn right and follow the lane until you reach a ford. Just after the ford turn
   left on to the Hangers Way, then turn left on to the next lane and right on to
   the footpath, just past the pond. Continue along the Hangers Way until you
   reach a dell (a small wooded hollow), which is the source of the River Rother.
   Leave the Hangers Way here, turning left on to the bridleway and following
   it alongside the stream to the lane.

4. Turn right and follow the lane down to Lower Green. Turn left here towards
   Empshott and then first right to Mabbotts. At the farm take the middle track,
   known as Standfast Lane, following it down a wooded gully to a metal gate.
   Go through the gate and continue across a large field. At the other side
   go through another metal gate, cross over the River Rother and follow the
   tree-lined route uphill to Church Lane.

5. Turn right down the lane and cross the main road with care. Continue along
   the path opposite through Cott's Shaw and up the hill behind Le Court
   Leonard Cheshire Home. Sitting on the site of an earlier ancient manor
   house, this Cheshire Home was the first of its kind to be founded by Sir
   Leonard Cheshire, himself a war hero, in the 1940s. Follow the path into an
   orchard, past an old hop kiln.

6. At the far end of the orchard, go through the deer fence and turn left up a
   steep path. Halfway up, bear right to follow the path through a field as it
   skirts around the hanger. When you reach the lane opposite Bradshott Hall
   turn left. At the top of the hill take the footpath on the right along the field
   edge, following the path as it wiggles down to and around a lake.

THE NATURAL HISTORY AND
ANTIQUITIES OF SELBORNE

Gilbert White (1720–1793) was born in Selborne and ordained as a deacon in 1749, inheriting his family home, The Wakes, in 1763, where he remained for the rest of his life. White's early enthusiasm for gardening led to a wider interest in the natural history of the surrounding countryside, resulting in his most famous work, *The Natural History and Antiquities of Selborne*, which has remained in print since its first publication in 1790. What made the book so special was that White based it on his observations of animals in their natural habitats, whereas most naturalists of the time concentrated on the indoor examination of dead specimens.

7. Having passed the lake, on the far side of the field, turn left along the fence – do not climb over the stile but follow the path along the valley. At the end of the conifer plantation, where the path divides, take the right-hand fork up the hanger slope and into the green lane. Bear left to pass the pond on your right and carry on to Sotherington Lane, where you turn right.

8. After a short way, the lane bends left and then right. Just before it bends right, take the footpath on the left-hand side and follow this round the edge of the field until you reach the playing fields. There are good views from here of Selborne Common, which is owned and managed by the National Trust.

9. Halfway along the hedge of the playing field, take the path to the right. Turn left on to the lane at the end, and then right on to the main road that takes you back into the village and your starting point. To reach Gilbert White's House and Gardens, simply continue along the road past The Selborne Arms and you will soon come to it on your right. The house also contains the Oates Collection, an exhibition focusing on two members of the Oates family, one of whom was Captain Lawrence Oates who accompanied Captain Scott on his ill-fated journey across Antarctica in 1910–12.

Courtesy of the South Downs Joint Committee and the South Downs National Park Authority. For more information go to www.southdowns.gov.uk

Destination Blackcap

LEWES AND OFFHAM

Starting out from the beautiful town of Lewes, this route takes you along the Sussex Ouse Valley Way before climbing steeply to the top of the downs. From here you follow the ridge to Blackcap, a stunning hilltop area owned by the National Trust that mainly lies within a Site of Special Scientific Interest (SSSI). A wide variety of flowers such as the yellow rockrose, musk orchid and honeysuckle can be found, while the diversity of tree species in the surrounding woodlands results in a glorious display of autumn colours. The hilltop is also the site of several burial mounds dating from the Bronze Age and Saxon times. Back in Lewes, your walk ends with a delightful stroll through the town's historic lanes and alleys.

DISTANCE:	12km (7½ miles) (circular)
TIME:	Allow 3½–4½ hours
LEVEL:	Moderate (with some steep climbs)
START/PARKING:	Lewes Railway Station (BN7 2UP). Parking available in station car park or in numerous other car parks. OS grid reference TQ416098 (OS Explorer map 122)
GETTING THERE:	*By car:* Follow A27 heading east from Brighton towards Eastbourne, and turn left on to A26 into Lewes *By public transport:* Train to Lewes Station
REFRESHMENTS:	Wide choice of pubs and cafés in Lewes or The Blacksmiths Arms, Uppham
LOCAL ATTRACTIONS:	Lewes Castle; Bentley Wildfowl and Motor Museum

DIRECTIONS

1. Turn right out of Lewes Station and at the crossroads turn right into Lansdown Place (B2193), continuing into Friars Walk. At the mini-roundabout turn right into Court Road, bearing left at the fork. Continue past the car park, bearing left into Railway Lane. At the T-junction turn right into Cliffe High Street and cross the bridge over the River Ouse.

2. After about 100m (110yd) turn left into a passageway and emerge into a car park. Follow the path along the wall around Harveys Brewery on the left and emerge on to the riverside path. Turn right, following the path under the road bridge and straight on until you reach open parkland. After about 300m (330yd) you reach Willey's footbridge over the river.

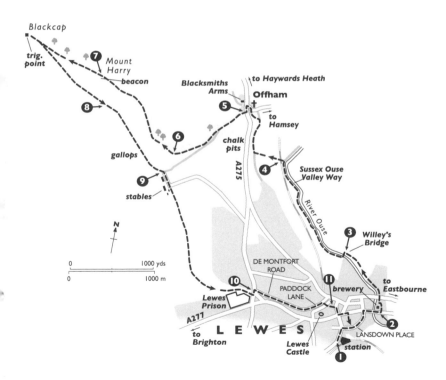

3. Cross the footbridge and turn right on to an unmade riverside path. Follow the river for about 1.5km (1 mile) along the Sussex Ouse Valley Way. As the river bears right towards Hamsey, cross the stile and turn left off the riverside path. Cross another stile and pass beneath the railway bridge into the water meadows, with water courses on either side and Offham chalk pits ahead. (Ignore another track that passes beneath the railway about 150m (165yd) earlier).

4. Walk through the meadows and after about 300m (330yd) cross the stile by the gate. Turn right on to the chalk track leading through the woodland below the roadway, which runs high up on the left. Follow the track for about 500m (550yd), climbing uphill to reach the road opposite Offham church, then turn left. When you reach the main road (A275) cross with care and turn left. Alternatively, a short detour to your right will bring you to The Blacksmiths Arms for some light refreshments.

5. Continuing your walk, after about 75m (82yd) turn right on to the bridleway heading into the woods. After 10m (11yd), fork right at the junction on to an ascending chalk track enclosed within fences. As the path begins to level out, you reach a gateway and post on the right. Pass through the gate into woodland and turn immediately left on to a path that initially follows in the same direction as the chalk track. After about 150m (165yd) the path bears left and climbs to open land, reaching a fence line and post.

6. Turn right on to the open land through the gap in the fence and follow the path, with the woodland on your right and open downland on your left. Pass through the gate and continue in the same direction, with the fence line now on your left and light woodland and scrub on your right. As the path ascends, you pass beneath power lines and through scrubland before re-emerging into more open downland. Continue along the path, heading towards the beacon on the horizon, and pass through another gate.

7. Upon reaching Mount Harry Beacon on the left, continue ahead on the clear wide path as it climbs towards Blackcap and the triangulation point at 206m

(676yd). After admiring the view, retrace your steps for about 100m (110yd) and fork half right on to another wide, gently descending path, heading directly towards the old racecourse buildings in the distance.

8. On reaching the gateway beneath the power lines, enter the scrub on the wide chalk track. This soon becomes narrower and more enclosed before emerging from the scrub with the gallops on your right. Follow the narrow track for about 500m (550ft) along the side of the gallops until you reach Suzy Smith Racing stables and buildings.

9. Pass through the gateway on to the tarmac road at the rear of the stables. On reaching the houses on the right, beyond the stables, bear left of the tall hedge on to a bridleway, leaving the tarmac road. Follow the path downhill for about 0.8km (½ mile) until you reach the rear walls of Lewes Prison on your right. Pass through the gateway on to the rough drive (Spital Road) and continue downhill to the main road (A275).

10. Cross the road with care, going half left into De Montfort Road, a residential street with Lewes Castle directly ahead. After about 400m (440yd) you reach a crossroad with Irelands Lane/Bradford Road; continue straight ahead here into the narrow one-way walled lane (Paddock Lane), descending gradually through the trees, with parkland on your left. On reaching Sycamore Lodge on the right, turn off the lane into enclosed path that ascends to New Road. Cross the road into another enclosed path that ascends and emerges opposite the Maltings (the East Sussex Record Office), to the left of the bowling green.

11. Continue ahead along the narrow street to the left of the Maltings to the junction, with The Lewes Arms on the left. Cross Castle Ditch Lane into the narrow lane opposite and after about 20m (22yd) reach Fisher Street. Cross into Market Lane and follow it until you reach Market Street. Turn right to the war memorial, then turn left and begin to descend School Hill. After about 50m (55yd) turn right into Church Twitten. Follow this narrow walled path as it descends to reach Friars Walk. At the bottom, turn right and make your way back to Lewes Station (or car park).

Courtesy of Per-Rambulations. For information
on other walks go to www.per-rambulations.co.uk

Fields, Copses and Hangers

LISS AND HAWKLEY

*Linking the easily accessible town of Liss with
the village of Hawkley, this lovely walk passes through
the East Hampshire Hangers (see special feature, page 39),
an area renowned for its steeply wooded hillsides. Forming a
figure-of-eight, the route starts out along an abandoned military
railway line, following the course of the River Rother, before
heading off across a tree nursery to a footbridge that takes you
over the A3 into open farmland. From here you skirt around the
hillside, past Crabtree Copse, until you meet the lane heading
west to Hawkley, where a detour takes you to the local pub
for refreshments. Your return journey takes you down
through a hanger and across the fields to the A3
crossing, and so back to Liss.*

DISTANCE:	11km (7 miles) (circular)
TIME:	Allow 3½–4½ hours
LEVEL:	Moderate (with one or two steep slopes)
START/PARKING:	Liss Station (GU33 7AA). Parking available in station car park or in Hill Brow Road, off Station Road. OS grid reference SU777278 (OS Explorer map 133)
GETTING THERE:	*By car:* Turn off A3, about 4.5km (3 miles) north east of Petersfield
	By public transport: Train to Liss Station
REFRESHMENTS:	The Hawkley Inn, Hawkley, or various pubs in Liss
LOCAL ATTRACTIONS:	Flora Twort Gallery and Bedales Historic Costume Collection, Petersfield

DIRECTIONS

1. From the railway station turn right over the level crossing and immediately right again along the Liss Riverside Railway Walk, following the dismantled railway line through a local nature reserve, alongside the River Rother. The railway used to connect the Longmoor Military Railway with Liss mainline but was closed in 1971. As you pass through the alder carr (wet woodland dominated by alder), look out for marshy plants such as the marsh marigold, which flowers from March through to the end of May.

2. After a short distance bear left and cross the footbridge over the river. Go through the gate and follow the path across the tree nursery and over the farm track until you reach the road at Burgates. Turn right and then next left up Church Street and follow the lane past St Peter's Church, much altered over the centuries but still maintaining its 13th-century tower. Where the road turns north, keep straight on down the footpath, crossing the footbridge over the dual carriageway of the A3.

3. On the far side, turn right and take the path that runs alongside the A3. Cross two fields then bear left away from the road, following the path along the field edge. Cross the stream and carry on until you reach Snailing Lane.

4. Turn right here and then left, following the footpath into a garden. Halfway along the hedge go through a small gate into the next garden, cutting across to the stile. Follow the line of stiles and waymarks uphill into a copse. When you emerge continue climbing straight ahead along a vague line of oak trees, crossing the field and the stile on the far side.

5. Just before the barn, at the edge of Crabtree Copse, you come to a grassy track. Turn right here, doubling back on yourself to follow the track downhill towards the river. Just before the river, turn left and follow the track up across the field and into a second field. Bear left halfway across the field and carry on to a gate that leads on to Standfast Lane.

6. Bear left and continue down the lane until you reach Mabbots Farm. Just past the farm, go left up the steep bank and through the gate on to the bridleway. Follow this around the field, emerging on to the lane by a small pond. Turn left down the lane past Uplands. You now have the option of making a short detour into Hawkley village where you can stop for refreshments. To do so, take the footpath off to the right across the field, then cross the road and go straight on to Hawkley village where you will find The Hawkley Inn on the right-hand side. Otherwise, continue along the lane towards the hanger.

7. Follow the road sharp left and down through the hanger, emerging once more into open farmland. The hummocky area in the fields below the hanger is the remains of a landslide that occurred in 1774, described by 18th-century naturalist Gilbert White in his book *The Natural History and Antiquities of*

Selborne: 'About fifty acres of land suffered from this violent convulsion; two houses were entirely destroyed; ... a hanging coppice was changed to naked rock; and some grass grounds and an arable field so broken and rifted by the chasms as to be rendered ... neither fit to plough or safe for pasturage.' Just past Slip Cottage take the footpath on your right, bearing left around the back of the farm buildings to reach a wide track. Bear right and go over another stile on to a wooded green lane.

8. Turn left along the lane, then shortly take the footpath on the right that runs between two fences. The path turns sharp right over a stile, where you will see another stile at right angles to it. Go over this and continue along the hedge bank. At the end of the field go over a stile, across the bridge and over another stile. Continue past the barn at Berrygrove Farm and on to the track.

9. At the end of the track bear slightly left to cross the field and pick up another track that takes you to the A3 bridge crossing at point 3 on the map. On the other side of the bridge, go diagonally right across the field to meet with another path, where you turn right to reach a road.

10. Cross the road and continue along the track opposite. Cross a second road and go through the kissing gate, heading for St Mary's Church, Liss. The path enters the churchyard at the side; go to the left of the church and out on to the main road. Turn right here to return to your starting point at Liss Station.

Courtesy of the South Downs Joint Committee and the South Downs National Park Authority. For more information go to www.southdowns.gov.uk

THE EAST HAMPSHIRE HANGERS

This walk lies among the East Hampshire Hangers, a distinctive landscape in which ancient woodlands cling to the steep slopes of chalk and upper greensand escarpments that lie between Petersfield in the south and Binsted in the north (greensand being an olive-green coloured sandstone). The name 'hanger' derives from an old English word 'hangra', meaning a wooded slope. Forming part of the South Downs National Park, the area contains many Sites of Special Scientific Interest (SSSIs) and nature reserves, and thanks to its outstanding beauty, rich wildlife and network of footpaths, including the 34km (21 mile) Hangers Way, proves highly popular with walkers.

Park and Woodland Walk

ANGMERING

*With a choice of routes, this pleasant walk starts
in the attractive village of Angmering – 6.5km (4 miles)
east of Worthing – with its well-preserved village square and fine
old buildings, some of which date back to the 14th century. From
here you head north of the A27 into the South Downs National
Park to explore the northern reaches of Angmering Parish, taking
in plantations, woodlands, fields and ponds along the way, and
bracing yourself for a surprise encounter with Highland cattle.
The shorter route passes through the fields and paddocks of historic
Angmering Park, while the longer woodland walk briefly joins
the Monarch's Way – a 990km (615 miles) long-distance path
that follows the route taken by Charles II in 1651 as he
fled his enemies after the Battle of Worcester.*

DISTANCE:	11km (7 miles) (circular) or shorter route of 5½ miles
TIME:	Allow 3½ – 4½ hours (shorter route: 2½ – 3½ hours)
LEVEL:	Moderate
START/PARKING:	Angmering village green, parking in front of shops or at station (BN16 4EF). OS grid reference SU068043 (OS Explorer map 121)
GETTING THERE:	*By car:* Turn off A27 just west of Worthing, on to B2225 Arundel Road
	By public transport: Train to Angmering Station
REFRESHMENTS:	The Lamb Inn, Angmering or The Woodman Arms, Hammerpot
LOCAL ATTRACTIONS:	Climping Sands at Littlehampton

DIRECTIONS

1. From the village green walk along Water Lane, passing The Lamb Inn on your left. After 0.8km (½ mile) turn left into Dapper's Lane and continue straight ahead. Pass under the A27 into Swillage Lane and carry on until you get to Swillage Pond. Local names provide evidence of how, in days gone by, the area was probably more marshy in nature than it is now. Swillage, for example, means 'wet, slushy place', which the area would have been when the water table was high.

2. Turn left beside the pond and follow the path along the line of an old hedge. Cross the bridge and turn left down the bridleway to Hammerpot. The name of the local pub – The Woodman Arms – reflects the fact that, in days gone by, many local people worked in the woodlands around this area. Indeed, at least one previous landlord was a retired forester.

3. If you are ready for refreshment, turn left down the lane to reach the pub. Otherwise, to continue your walk, turn right through the hamlet and continue alongside the A27 until you reach a stile. Cross over the stile and walk across the field and over another stile. When you reach the road, turn right and continue along the road until you come to a footpath on your left that leads into the woods. Take this footpath through Butler's Copse to The Dover car park, emerging at a junction of paths and roads.

4. From the corner of The Dover car park continue straight ahead along the road which soon changes into a stony track. Highland cattle can sometimes be seen grazing in the paddocks on either side of the track. Follow the track round to the right, past The Dover Cottage, and continue straight ahead at the next path junction until you reach Angmering Park Cottages.

5. You now have a choice of route. To take the longer walk through the woodlands, go straight to direction 7 below. Otherwise, for the shorter walk through the parkland, take the footpath to the right and walk through the paddocks and across the estate access road leading to Angmering Park Stud Farm. Continue along the path, following the field edge and carrying straight on at the four-way path junction beside the copse.

6. At the next junction follow the bridleway to the right. Where it bears round to the right take the path to the left, with an open field on your left and woodland on your right. Continue straight ahead until you reach the pond at Swillage Lane (point 2/11 on the map). From here, retrace your steps back to Angmering village, following direction 11 below.

7. For the longer walk, carry straight ahead at Angmering Park Cottages and follow the track through the beech plantation bordered in places by Douglas firs. The grassy verge on either side of the track contains many plants, including wild basil, nettle-leaved bellflower and fleabane. In places along this walk you will come across lighter coppice woodland: notice the contrast between this and the dense beech plantations. Coppicing – cutting back the tree stems every few years – lets through more light, allowing a wider range of woodland plants to grow.

8. At the junction of the paths turn right and keep going uphill along Monarch's Way, passing a pine plantation on your left. At the next junction continue straight ahead, passing Keepers Cottage on your right. Continue straight ahead, staying on the bridleway and ignoring the first path off to the right. Throughout the woodland there are ruins of cottages and wells, indicating that the area was once more populated than it is today.

9. At the next junction make a right turn where the bridleways fork. Shortly after, turn right again and follow the track as it bears around to the left. Continue straight ahead across the next path junctions until you emerge from the woods at Selden Farm.

10. Beyond the farm, take the footpath to the right along the field edge, through a copse and bear left across the corner of another field. Walk through the woodland and emerge into Swillage Lane, turning left to take you back to the pond at point 2/11 on the map.

11. To return to Angmering, continue straight ahead down Swillage Lane, under the A27 and along Dapper's Lane. Turn right at the bottom along Water Lane to take you back to the village green.

Courtesy of Angmering Parish Council. For more information go to www.angmeringparishcouncil.gov.uk

ANGMERING PARK

There has been a park at Angmering since at least 1279. In the Middle Ages this would essentially have been a game reserve – an area in which deer were kept to provide sport and meat. Today the estate is managed for forestry, shooting, agriculture and wildlife, in addition to which there is a stud farm and an internationally renowned racing yard. One of the more unusual animals to be found grazing in the paddocks is Highland cattle – special enclosures that extend into the woodland have been built in order to protect these beasts from the hot summer sunshine.

Chanctonbury Ring Hill Fort

STEYNING AND WASHINGTON

*This scenic walk starts off in the historic town
of Steyning, well known as one of the most picturesque
towns in Sussex, with its fine Norman church and wealth
of timber-framed buildings. From here you climb the steep
escarpment of the South Downs to join up with the South Downs
Way, which takes you to Chanctonbury Ring, an Iron Age hill fort
from where you can admire the spectacular views. On leaving
the ring the route descends steeply towards the village of
Washington, giving you the option of extending your walk
to visit the local hostelry before making your way back
to your starting point.*

DISTANCE: 11km (7 miles) (circular) or 14.5km (9 miles)
with extension
TIME: Allow 3½–4½ hours (with extension: 4½–5½ hours)
LEVEL: Moderate (with a steep ascent and descent)

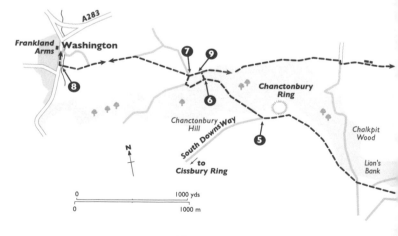

START/PARKING: Car park at Fletchers Croft, beside the Steyning Centre in Steyning (BN44 3XZ). OS grid reference TQ178112 (OS Explorer map 121)

GETTING THERE: *By car:* Turn off A24, about 19km (12 miles) south of Horsham, on to A283, then turn right down B2135 to Steyning
By public transport: Train to Shoreham-by-Sea then catch Brighton and Hove bus no. 2A, or train to Pulborough, then catch bus no. 100 to Burgess Hill, alighting at Bamber Road, Steyning

REFRESHMENTS: A selection of pubs and cafés in Steyning, or The Frankland Arms, Washington

LOCAL ATTRACTIONS: St Mary's House and Gardens; Steyning Museum

DIRECTIONS

1. From the car park, walk towards the Steyning Centre, then turn right down School Lane, passing between the school buildings. At the junction turn left down Church Street to the staggered crossroads and mini roundabout. Cross the road with care and go down the road (almost) opposite, alongside The White Horse pub. At White Horse Square turn right. Shortly afterwards turn left, passing a police station and entering a playing field. Head diagonally across the field to the far right corner, exiting via a gate.

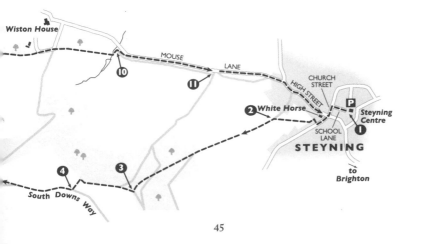

2. Turn left up the track and pass through two more gates to enter a more open area and then continue straight ahead up the grassy slope, ignoring the path on the left. After another gate immediately turn right (not downhill) and almost immediately join another path coming uphill; turn left here and continue climbing.

3. At the edge of the woods near the top of the hill, bear right on to another path coming from the left, keeping the trees on your right. Ignoring the path down to the right, follow the path round the edge of the wood, bearing left across the field to reach the South Downs Way.

4. Turn right and follow the South Downs Way, admiring the views to your left of Cissbury Ring – one of the largest Middle Iron Age hill forts in Europe, dating back to 250BC – and the coast beyond. Ignore the side paths to left and right and continue following the signs for the South Downs Way, keeping the woodland on your right. At a gate and cattle grid, carry straight on, with Chanctonbury Ring clearly ahead of you. Continue uphill until you reach the hill fort, from where there are far-reaching views, making this a good place for a picnic.

5. Shortly after leaving the ring turn half right, leaving the South Downs Way, and walk down to a gate. Pass through the gate and walk steeply down the grassy slope through the woods. Some way down, after a clearing, is an unmarked path off to the right, which descends to a track.

6. If you want to do the shorter walk (and do not wish to go to Washington for refreshment) turn right down this path, turning right again at the bottom on to the track (go straight to direction 9 below). For the extension to Washington, carry straight on along the main path, passing through a gate and, after a short rise, descending to a junction of paths. Drop down to a lower path and turn right, shortly arriving at a small clearing with four gates.

7. To the left are a field gate and a smaller gate, and to the right a pair of field gates (the right-hand one into the woods being the route back to Steyning). For Washington, go through the small gate and follow the footpath half left across the field (do not follow the path along the field edge). Cross a stile and continue along the path until you reach a track. Bear left here and pass through a gate, carrying straight ahead on the grass when the track turns right into a farm. Follow the path over stiles and steps until you reach the road into Washington.

8. Turn right and walk up the road to The Frankland Arms for some light refreshments, returning by the same route to the clearing with the four gates (point 7 on the map). Take the right-hand field gate and follow the track into the woods. Just after the old gateposts, near the brow of a rise, you join up with the shorter route on a path coming in from the right.

9. Continue on the main track (turning right if you took the shorter route), passing through an old iron field gate and past a house on your right just before reaching a minor road. Turn right and then left over a stile, passing some farm buildings and behind Wiston House on your left. Cross two stiles and go under a high footbridge. Where the tarmac track turns left, keep right and walk between the trees and a fence to a stile. Cross and turn right to another stile, then cross a tiny stream.

10. At the field corner, you can either go ahead and turn right on to Mouse Lane or turn right to walk parallel to the lane, continuing to a crossing path via a stile and some steps where you turn left to join Mouse Lane. Note the stone plaque on the far left bank (the original is in Steyning Museum).

11. Turn right on to Mouse Lane (although in fact you are carrying straight on) and follow the lane down to the High Street. Walk along the High Street until you reach The White Horse pub, where you turn left and retrace your steps back to the start of the walk.

Courtesy of Steyning and District Community Partnership.
For more information go to www.steyningsouthdowns.com

Duncton and Woolavington Downs

DUNCTON AND EAST LAVINGTON

This exhilarating walk climbs steadily through pleasant woodland to the top of the South Downs, affording fine views along the way. Starting out in the picturesque village of Duncton, the route takes you past the beautiful Duncton Mill Fishery, an old lime kiln and a chalk quarry, one of the few still being worked. Returning past Seaford College, you have the opportunity of visiting the 13th-century church where Samuel Wilberforce, or 'Soapy Sam', lies buried. Back at your starting point, spare a moment to look at the The Cricketers' inn sign, which shows local cricketing hero James Dean, one-time landlord of the inn and known affectionately as 'Joyous Jemmy'.

DISTANCE:	9.5km (6 miles) (circular)
TIME:	3–4 hours
LEVEL:	Moderate with some steep climbs
START/PARKING:	Park in lay-by in front of The Cricketer's pub (GU28 0LB). OS grid reference SU960171 (OS Explorer map 121)
GETTING THERE:	*By car:* About 6.5km (4 miles) south of Petworth on the A285
	By public transport: Train to Chichester, then bus no. 99 from cathedral to Beechwood Lane, Duncton
REFRESHMENTS:	The Cricketers, Duncton
LOCAL ATTRACTIONS:	Petworth House

DIRECTIONS

1. With your back to the pub turn right and take the concrete path between the hedgerow and the main road, heading north. After about 50m (55yd) turn right down Dye House Lane, following the bridleway sign. Walk past Wild Cherries bed and breakfast as the track drops and swings right. After crossing a stream follow the track as it climbs to the delightful setting of Duncton Mill Trout Fishery. Continue straight ahead here, carrying on uphill until you reach the public road where you turn right.

2. From here there are views of Seaford College ahead and of the aerial on Bexleyhill away to the right. On reaching the main A285 turn sharp left and follow the bridleway sign up to a metal gate. Pass through a wooden gate to one side and begin climbing gently up through the trees, following the path as it swings left to reach an old hidden lime kiln. The path now zigzags right then left uphill before levelling out after about 10 minutes.

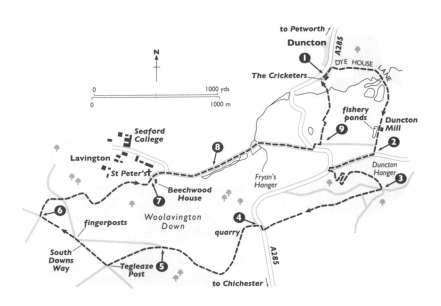

3. When you reach the wooden post with the eight blue direction arrows, turn right and then take the left hand of two paths, which heads slightly more steeply uphill. Ignoring a bridleway off to the left, continue climbing straight ahead until the path levels out and emerges on to the north slope of an open field. Cross the field to the main road and turn right, keeping to the right-hand side.

4. After just 50m (55yd) turn left, crossing the road with care and walking up the tarmac drive into the Duncton Minerals site. At the metal gate entrance to the quarry swing left and take the broad track heading uphill, following the green arrow. At one point there is a good view of the deep quarry down to the right, illustrating clearly that these hills are almost entirely chalk. Continue to follow the track as it levels off and opens out.

5. Bear left at the fork in the path and continue gently uphill until you reach the crossing of the South Downs Way at Tegleaze Post. Turn right along the national trail as it heads westwards, going slightly downhill and passing a unique four-armed fingerpost – each arm indicating a different 'right of way'. Carry straight on, past a second (three-armed) fingerpost, until you meet a broad crossing track.

THROWING A LIGHT ON LIME

Lime has always been important in both building and farming. It was produced in kilns like the one found on this walk by burning the chalk from the South Downs. The resulting calcium oxide is a nasty, unstable substance more commonly known as quicklime, which can be stabilized by adding water to produce calcium hydroxide or 'slaked lime'. Mixed with sand and ash this makes a strong mortar, and can also be used to correct acidity in the soil. If a stick of quicklime is heated in an oxyhydrogen flame it gives off an intense white light. This was once widely used for lighting the stage in theatres and music halls, and is better known as 'limelight'.

6. Turn right and follow the path across the open field to the tree line. As you enter the trees the path drops more steeply; keep to the right-hand track here, leaving a wooden rail fence on your left. Walk carefully down the hill towards Seaford College and on reaching a high brick wall carry on straight ahead, keeping the wall to your left. Follow the path as it swings left, remaining close to the wall, and after 100m (110yd) look for a wooden gate on the right bearing a sign for Beechwood House.

7. Carry on for another 20m (22yd) and, on reaching a wooden fence on your left, turn sharp left to follow a narrow path up a short flight of stone steps into the churchyard of St Peter's Church, Lavington. Against the far wall you will find the gravestone of Samuel Wilberforce, one-time Bishop of Oxford, later of Winchester. It was perhaps his ability to be 'all things to all men' that earned him the nickname 'Soapy Sam'. Retrace your steps to the main track and continue along it as it becomes a tarmac lane and drops downhill.

8. You soon pass Willow Cottage with its crystal clear, spring-fed lake and beautiful display of daffodils in March. Follow the drive all the way out to the main road. Carefully cross the road to the fingerpost opposite, beside a low wall. Turn left towards a derelict brick and flint building and just before reaching it turn right, following the yellow arrow.

9. After 25m (27yd) turn left, heading uphill with a high flint wall on your left. You soon reach an open field with views of the fishery ponds to your right. Follow the path down the left side of the field, keeping the hedgerow to your left. At the end of the hedgerow cross a stile to the left and continue in much the same direction across the centre of the next field (aiming just right of a telegraph pole). When you reach the trees, cross over the stile and follow the path as it drops down to a delightful plank bridge over a stream. Climb up the other side towards the buildings, crossing another stile to emerge at the lay-by and the welcoming sight of The Cricketers inn.

Courtesy of Footprints of Sussex. For more information go to www.footprintsofsussex.co.uk

Poets, Parks and Waterfalls

BIGNOR AND SUTTON

This delightful walk starts out in the Lord's Piece, an area of heathland sheltered by the South Downs, which is vitally important as the last native site for the field cricket. The route then takes you across fields and woodlands through Bignor Park, where the poet and novelist Charlotte Smith once lived, and on to the village of Bignor, with its peaceful 11th-century church, famous Yeoman's House – a 15th-century timber-framed hall house – and nearby Roman villa. Passing through a narrow valley with a waterfall, you return via Sutton village where The White Horse Inn provides a welcome break for thirsty walkers.

DISTANCE:	8km (5 miles) (circular)
TIME:	2½–3½ hours
LEVEL:	Moderate (with stiles and two short hills)
START/PARKING:	The Lord's Piece car park on minor road between Burton Mill and Fittleworth, about 4.5km (3 miles) south east of Petworth (nearby post code: RH20 1ES). OS grid reference SU990174 (OS Explorer map 121)
GETTING THERE:	*By car:* From Petworth, head towards Pulborough on A283, turning right on to B2138 at Fittleworth. After 1.5km (1 mile), turn right to Coates and continue until you reach car park on left
	By public transport: see www.traveline.info
REFRESHMENTS:	The White Horse Inn, Sutton
LOCAL ATTRACTIONS:	Bignor Roman Villa; Parkham House and Gardens

DIRECTIONS

1. Heading out from the car park, pass through the kissing gate to the right of the information board and take the middle of three paths across the centre of the common. Keep walking along this sandy path in an easterly direction, climbing the small rise with tall pines immediately to your left. If you now look behind you, you will get a particularly fine view of the South Downs, dominated by Barlavington Down. Follow the path as it drops down between chestnut trees to reach a crossing bridleway.

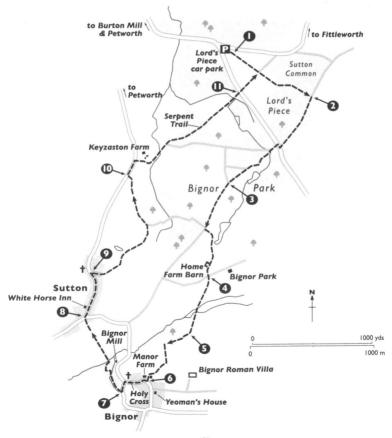

A Poet's Paradise

Bignor Park was once home to the highly successful novelist and poet Charlotte Smith (1749–1806), who was brought up in a modest house on the estate. Wed at the tender age of 15, she had 12 children by her profligate husband Benjamin, who ended up in debtor's prison where Charlotte joined him and wrote her first book of poetry. Among her best-known novels are *Emmeline* and *The Old Manor House*, which were much admired by Sir Walter Scott. The current house was built in the 1820s by John Hawkins, a Cornish tin miner, and was acquired by writer and traveller Lord Mersey in 1926, since when it has been lovingly cared for by his family.

2. Pass through the kissing gate and turn right, following the broad drover's track for about 600m (660yd) until you meet a public road. Turn right and then, after just 20m (22yd), turn left through a gate into Bignor Park. After about 50m (55yd), bear left at the fork and follow the path slightly uphill. At the next fork keep left again, shortly afterwards ignoring a bridleway to the right.

3. Continue ahead with more open fields now on either side. After 400m (440yd), where the track begins to swing right, turn left on to the crossing path, passing through a kissing gate into an open field. Walk to the right corner where a second kissing gate leads on to a broad farm track. Turn left towards the buildings. After a large gate the track becomes surfaced and passes in front of the beautiful Home Farm Barn to meet the main drive through Bignor Park. The estate was once the home of novelist and poet, Charlotte Smith (see special feature, left).

4. Cross straight over through a five-bar gate into the field and turn half right, heading just to the right of the large oak tree. Keep this line as you drop down towards the trees and look carefully for the yellow footpath arrow leading down to a footbridge over the stream. On crossing this, turn right and climb to the high right-hand corner of the field.

5. Cross a stile and continue climbing through the trees; the path opens out on to a level field with lovely views of Bignor village. Turn right along the edge of the field and follow the fingerposts left and then right towards the farm buildings. Carefully follow the signs through Manor Farm

to the public road and turn right towards the church. (From here you can detour to visit the Yeoman's House and Bignor Roman Villa.)

6. Pass the church of Holy Cross and turn left downhill at the junction, with Ivy Cottage to your right. On passing Charmans, turn right and follow the fingerposted footpath through a gate to pass behind the house.

7. As you walk down into the glade, look to your left for one of the few waterfalls in Sussex. Continue over two plank bridges, emerging to a lovely view of Bignor Mill. Crossing a more substantial bridge and stile, follow the path as it climbs up a grassy slope to a gap in the hedge. Walk across the middle of the next field to a narrow path leading into Sutton by the White Horse Inn.

8. Continue northwards along the Petworth road with the pub to your left. Pass the village hall and telephone kiosk (ignoring a path here) and as Sutton church comes clearly into view turn right in front of Old School House.

9. Follow the surfaced road downhill and take the left fork on to a grassy track leading to a stile. The path through the bushes soon emerges into an open field with good views to the north of Petworth and the Greensand Ridge. Continue down the right side of the field where a kissing gate leads into a larger open field. Cross diagonally to a fingerpost at the bottom end of a tree line and walk past it to a second post with yellow footpath arrows. Here turn half left into the corner of the field. Cross the stile and follow a wire fence on your right to reach a plank bridge and stile. Cross the middle of the next grazing field towards a delightful thatched cottage where two further stiles lead behind the building on to the public road.

10. Turn right and, after 200m (220yd), turn right again into Keyzaston Farm, following the Serpent Trail. At the farmhouse follow the track around to the right as it swings downhill and begins to curve left. After 150m (165yd), where the path forks, keep left and follow the bridleway through woods to the public road.

11. Cross the road with care and pass through the gate opposite into Lord's Piece. Turn left through the grazing Exmoor ponies to return to the car park.

Courtesy of Footprints of Sussex. For more information go to www.footprintsofsussex.co.uk

Ditchling Beacon to Devil's Dyke

With its stunning views across the Weald to the north and the English Channel to the south, this fantastic walk takes you along one of the most spectacular stretches of the South Downs Way. Starting from Ditchling Beacon, a famed beauty spot, the route crosses the top of the Downs to a pair of windmills, from where you have the option of descending to Clayton village to view some world-renowned frescoes. Continuing with the walk, you follow the undulating landscape to Devil's Dyke, a dry, V-shaped valley where refreshments await you. This walk is designed to make full use of the 'Breeze up to the Downs' bus service from Brighton; alternatively, car-users can retrace their steps at any point along the way.

DISTANCE:	8km (5 miles) (linear)
TIME:	Allow 2½–3½ hours
LEVEL:	Moderate to strenuous (with steep climbs and descents)
START/PARKING:	Ditchling Beacon, parking in car park (nearby post

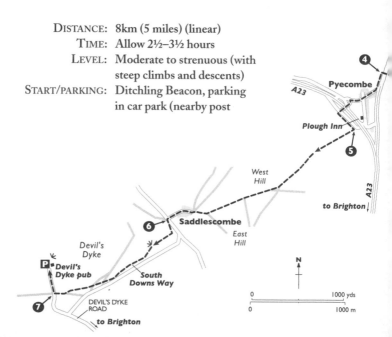

code: BN6 8RH). OS grid reference
TQ332113 (OS Explorer map 122)

GETTING THERE: *By car:* Turn north off A27, just north
of Brighton, on to Ditchling Road
By public transport: Train to Brighton
then 'Breeze up to the Downs' bus no. 79
to Ditchling Beacon, returning to Brighton
on bus no. 77 from Devil's Dyke (check online
at www.brighton-hove.gov.uk for details; show
rail tickets for 2-for-1 offer)

REFRESHMENTS: The Plough Inn, Pyecombe, or Devil's Dyke pub

LOCAL ATTRACTIONS: Medieval frescoes in St John the Baptist Church,
Clayton

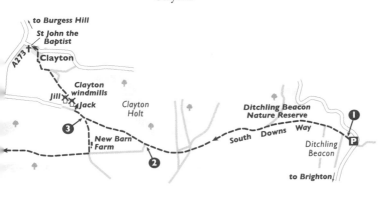

DIRECTIONS

1. At 248m (814ft), Ditchling Beacon is one of the highest points in the South
Downs, for which reason it was a defensive stronghold in the early Iron Age.
You can still see some of the fort's banks and ditches today. As the name
suggests, it was also a beacon site in Elizabethan times – one of a chain that
could be used to warn of imminent invasion. From the car park, follow the
blue acorn markers along the South Downs Way, keeping the sea on your left.

2. After about 1.5km (1 mile), just before you reach the Clayton windmills, you
pass Clayton Holt on your right. This ancient woodland on the steep northern

escarpment is estimated to be 10,000 years old and is worth a diversion off the main path. Returning to the South Downs Way, continue along the path towards Clayton windmills. The landscape here is undulating and many of the mounds are not natural features but 'tumuli', or ancient burial mounds.

3. The windmills are affectionately called Jack and Jill after the famous nursery rhyme, and were probably named in the 1920s by day-trippers travelling down from London. Jack is not open to the public, but Jill is open on Sundays during the summer months. A detour past the windmills takes you down to Clayton village, where the Saxon church of St John the Baptist contains a series of world-renowned, early 12th-century frescos. Depicting the Last Judgement, these comprise one of England's most complete sets of early mediaeval church wall-paintings. After exploring the windmills, and/or making the detour down to Clayton, return to point 3 on the map, from where you can see the northern edge of Brighton. Follow the South Downs Way heading south past New Barn Farm, then turn right and follow the path through the golf course until you reach the A273.

4. Cross the road with care and follow the path opposite as it runs parallel to the road before bearing right to join up with a lane leading into Pyecombe. This small village is steeped in ancient downland shepherding history, and gave its name to the distinctive shepherd's crook, known as the 'Pyecombe Hook', which was crafted in the old Pyecombe Forge and proved highly popular with shepherds across the Sussex Downs in the latter part of the last millennium. Follow the lane down to the crossroads, where a left-hand turn down Church Lane takes you to the historic Plough Inn for some well-earned refreshments. Otherwise, continue straight ahead along Church Hill, following the route across the bridge over the A23 London Road and left down the lane.

5. Just past the large buildings on your right, bear right and continue straight ahead along the track. From here on you are on National Trust land once more and the landscape quickly becomes stunning again. Follow the path as it wends is way up and over the downs to the historic hamlet of Saddlescombe, with its 16th-century manor farm. Follow the lane

WILDLIFE WATCH

There is a rich abundance of plant and animal life to be found along this walk. Lady's bedstraw, devil's bit scabious, squinancywort, salad burnet, ribwort plantain and burnet saxifrage are just a few of the quirkily named wildflowers that thrive along the South Downs ridge, while orchid species include the bee, fragrant, common spotted and pyramidal orchids, best spotted in bloom in late spring and early summer. Listen out for skylarks as they soar overhead. If you're lucky you may also catch sight of warblers, linnets, yellowhammers, grey partridge and corn buntings along the route. The best places for spotting butterflies on the Downs are steep slopes that do not have a history of ploughing and farming, such as those at Devil's Dyke. Three species of blue can be found: the chalkhill blue and Adonis blue can be distinguished from the common blue by their chequered wing tips, while the Adonis blue is a deeper sky blue colour than the chalkhill blue.

through Saddlescombe, taking a quick signposted detour to the farm's donkey wheel and well, which is thought to be 400 years old.

6. Cross the road at the end of the village with care and follow the South Downs Way to Devil's Dyke, stopping to admire the views along the way. This large dry valley – the largest in Britain – has thrilled day-trippers since Victorian times, when there was a fairground here and a cable car crossing the hillside, served by a small train line that brought visitors up from Brighton. Devil's Dyke is also the site of a prehistoric hill fort and settlement. Today you'll see hang-gliders catching thermals and updrafts from the valley slopes.

7. Where the path crosses Devil's Dyke Road, turn right and follow the lane up to The Devil's Dyke public house for refreshments. From here you can either choose to retrace your steps to your starting point or catch the number 77 bus back into Brighton.

Courtesy of The National Trust. For more information go to www.nationaltrust.org.uk or telephone 01243 814554 for a copy of 'Stroll the South Downs' walks pack.

Burpham Down Circuit

BURPHAM, WEPHAM AND THE NORFOLK CLUMP

*This peaceful walk along quiet country lanes and
well-defined tracks takes you across the wide-open expanse
of Burpham Down, from where you get splendid views of Arundel
Castle, a mere 3km (2 miles) to the south-west. Your walk starts
out at the picturesque church of St Mary the Virgin, in Burpham,
where you can seek out the graves of famous residents and view
a leper's window. From here you climb gently through open fields
towards the highest point of the downs, marked by a distinctive
group of trees known as the Norfolk Clump. Returning to
your starting point, your efforts are rewarded by
refreshments at the local inn.*

DISTANCE:	8km (5 miles) (circular)
TIME:	2½–3½ hours
LEVEL:	Moderate (with stiles and two short hills)
START/PARKING:	Car park beside recreation ground in Burpham village (BN18 9RR). OS grid reference TQ039088 (OS Explorer map 121)
GETTING THERE:	*By car:* Turn north off A27 Chichester/Brighton road, just east of Arundel, to Warningcamp and Burpham
	By public transport: see www.traveline.info
REFRESHMENTS:	The George and Dragon, Burpham
LOCAL ATTRACTIONS:	Amberley Chalk Pits Museum

DIRECTIONS

1. From the car park walk past The George and Dragon pub, cross the road with care and walk into the churchyard of St Mary the Virgin, opposite, where Reverend Tickner Edwardes and author Mervyn Peake lie buried (see special feature, page 62). The church dates from 1180 and contains an unusual leper's window, which was added in the Middle Ages when an isolation hospital was established near here on a remote part of the downs. The lepers were not allowed inside the church and received a blessing through this window while kneeling outside the church. (From the porch, walk a little to your right to see the low lancet window, where the chancel joins the nave.) Continue walking around the church, ignoring a path over the church wall, and exit the churchyard via the north gate on to the tarmac road.

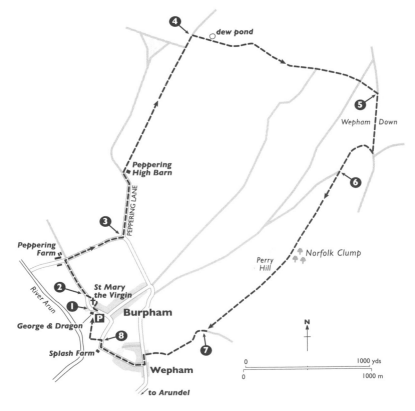

BURPHAM'S LITERARY PAST

Burpham has a rich literary past, its most famous resident being the author, poet and artist Mervyn Peake (1911–1968), whose Gormenghast trilogy may have been inspired by views of Arundel Castle. Another resident and one-time rector of Burpham, Reverend Tickner Edwardes, wrote a number of books on natural history and local folklore. His best-known work is *The Lore of the Honey-Bee* – bees being one of his great obsessions. Author and essayist John Cowper Powys (1872–1963) lived here around the turn of the last century and is best remembered for his novels, such as *A Glastonbury Romance*.

2. Keep right along the road, from where you will get good views of Arundel Castle (behind you to your left). At Peppering Farm turn right, following the tarmac road between the telegraph poles. At the next road junction, by the grassy triangle, turn left down Peppering Lane, following the bridleway signs. The four unusual trees ahead to your right are Alp pines with ivy growing on them.

3. After 400m (440yd) you will reach a group of converted farm buildings; just beyond them turn right, following a yellow footpath sign that takes you gently uphill. The path soon becomes a broad chalk path or 'bostal', as it is known locally. After about 15 minutes of gentle uphill walking you reach a dense clump of bushes on your left with a fingerpost giving a choice of directions.

4. At the fingerpost turn right, heading slightly downhill, and after 100m (110yd) you pass a large dew pond to your left. Dew ponds were constructed to provide water for animals grazing on the downs, there being no streams or rivers up here. Once excavated, the hollow would be lined with straw and then clay, and left overnight. As the surface of the clay became colder than the surrounding earth, dew would form in the pond. The majority of the water, however, came from rainwater, although legend would have it that, because of the dew, these ponds never ran dry. Follow the track as it descends into the valley and climbs more steeply on the far side to meet a crossing bridleway near the top of the hill.

5. Pass ahead through the farm gate and turn half right to continue climbing more gently to a concrete track. A few metres further on, upon reaching the gate, take care to leave the concrete track by turning hard right, almost doubling back on yourself. The path goes very slightly downhill and constantly curves left. You should soon be heading southwest back towards Burpham with the Arun Valley ahead and to your right. The village you can see across the valley is South Stoke with the spire of St Leonard's Church just visible.

6. Ignore a fingerpost pointing down to the right and continue to climb gently until you reach a clump of trees to the left of the path. This is the Norfolk Clump and at 122m (400ft) the highest point on the walk. Continue along the now grassy route as it descends slowly to a metal gate besides some summer sheep pens. Carry straight on to reach a fingerpost with a stile to the left. There is a fine view of Burpham village from here. The name 'Burpham' comes from two Saxon words meaning 'village hill fort', and the outline of the defensive mound is quite clear from this viewpoint.
(If the two words are reversed you get 'Hamburg', a city whose name has exactly the same meaning.)

7. Go to the right of a small clump of hawthorn trees and head downhill to pass over a stile beside an iron gate. The path swings half right and drops more steeply to reach the public road at Wepham. Turn left past an old granary and then take the first road to the right, heading more steeply downhill.

8. At the bottom of the hill, immediately after the bend at Splash Farm, take the narrow path to the left, heading uphill through the trees. At the top of the hill cross a stile into an open field. Cross straight over to a second stile and turn right past the children's playground to the welcoming sight of The George and Dragon pub.

Courtesy of Footprints of Sussex. For more information go to www.footprintsofsussex.co.uk

Round Tower Ramble

SOUTHEASE, PIDDINGHOE, TELSCOMBE AND RODMELL

*Starting out on the Sussex Ouse Valley Way, just
south of Lewes, this lovely walk takes you along the
riverbank and through fields and downlands to view four
ancient churches and three unusual round towers. Along the way
you visit the beautifully preserved village of Telscombe, where the
roadside banks are filled with glorious displays of daffodils in
springtime, and on to Rodmell, with its still-operational forge
and welcoming public house. Here you have the opportunity to
visit Monk's House, once the rural retreat of novelist Virginia
Woolf and her husband Leonard, and now owned by the
National Trust (check online for
opening times).*

DISTANCE: 8km (5 miles) (circular) with 1.5km
(1 mile) extension

TIME: Allow 2½–3½ hours

LEVEL: Moderate (with some steep climbs)

START/PARKING: St Peter's Church, Southease (BN7 3HX),
4.5km (3 miles) north of Newhaven, parking
on green. OS grid reference TQ432052
(OS Explorer map 123)

GETTING THERE: *By car:* Follow A27 heading east towards
Eastbourne, turning off on to A26 to
Newhaven, then turning right into Southease
By public transport: Take train to Southease
Station and walk to point 2 on map

REFRESHMENTS: The Abergavenny Arms, Rodmell

LOCAL ATTRACTIONS: Monk's House (National Trust); Firle Place

DIRECTIONS

1. The walk starts at the 13th-century church of St Peter, one of only three Sussex churches to have a round tower. From here, walk downhill past the green and bear right on to the lane leading down towards the river, which once flowed close to the village until it was canalized 400m (440yd) away. Upon reaching Southease bridge, do not cross over; instead, turn right through the gate on to the Sussex Ouse Valley Way.

2. Walk south along the riverbank path for about 1.5km (1 mile). At this point the river is tidal and still navigable by smaller craft as far as Lewes. Where the path converges with the road near Dean's Farm, cross the stile and the road,

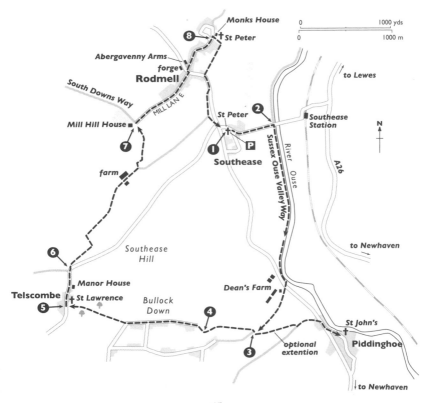

65

with care, and enter the driveway opposite, to the left of the entrance gates. Follow the drive for about 600m (660yd) until you reach a waymark, at which point the Sussex Ouse Valley Way heads left towards Piddinghoe village.

3. You can now choose to make a short detour to view the ancient church at Piddinghoe, the second church on the walk to have an unusual round tower. Turn left and follow the path up the grassy bank to a gateway, then continue to follow the waymarks into the village, returning the same way. This detour adds about 1.5km (1 mile) to your journey. Otherwise, carry straight on for about 20m (22yd), then turn right off the driveway and continue ahead, inside of the hedge in the field, until the path begins to climb half right to the corner of the field. Pass through the gateway into the larger field and follow the path diagonally right, climbing to the top corner of the field.

4. Turn right and then left through the gate on to an enclosed path to emerge on to a track by some houses. Follow the track with the houses on your left for about 800m (875yd). Turn right off the track on to a path that takes you across open downland and into light woodland, emerging by the church in the unspoilt village of Telscombe (see special feature, opposite). The ancient church of St Lawrence has Norman work dating from the early 1100s, with additions later that century including the tower – square this time – crowned by its Sussex cap. One of Telscombe's infamous residents was James Lulham who, in 1819, became the last man in England to be hanged for sheep stealing.

5. Turn right along the road and walk through village, passing the Manor House on your right, with its flint-faced round tower. Now owned by the National Trust, the house dates from the 18th century, with Victorian alterations and additions. Although the tower is called the Saxon Tower, it too dates from the 19th century. At the top of the hill, about 200m (220yd) after leaving the houses of the village behind you, the road bears right. Turn left here on to the path that heads downhill through open downland.

6. Follow the clear path as it descends gradually to meet a field boundary. Bear left here and then right and continue along the rough track to reach the farm buildings. Walk through the farm to meet up with the South Downs Way. Turn left on to this path and follow it up the steep hill to reach Mill Lane and the entrance to Mill Hill House on the left.

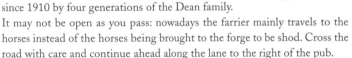

7. Leave the South Downs Way for now and turn right along the lane, following it for over 0.8km (½ mile) until you reach the main road at Rodmell, opposite The Abergavenny Arms where a drop of light refreshment may be in order. The old forge opposite the pub has been worked since 1910 by four generations of the Dean family. It may not be open as you pass: nowadays the farrier mainly travels to the horses instead of the horses being brought to the forge to be shod. Cross the road with care and continue ahead along the lane to the right of the pub.

8. After about 0.4km (¼ mile) you pass the entrance to Rodmell church on the right, beyond which stands a weatherboarded cottage. This is Monks House, the last home of the innovative novelist Virginia Woolf, who lived here with her husband, Leonard, until she tragically ended her life in 1941 by drowning herself in the River Ouse. The house now belongs to the National Trust. Turn along the enclosed path leading to the 12th-century church of St Peter, then follow the waymarks for the Sussex Ouse Valley Way, which will take you back on to the main road where you turn left for the return route to Southease.

Courtesy of Per-Rambulations. For similar walks go to www.per-rambulations.co.uk

Telscombe Time Warp

Protected from new development, Telscombe owes its state of preservation to two men: Ambrose Gorham and Ernest Thornton-Smith. Gorham, a retired bookmaker, became Lord of the Manor at the end of the 19th century. He proved a generous benefactor to the village, providing a water supply in 1909 (prior to this villagers had to collect water from their roofs!) and electricity in 1930. When he died in 1933 he left his land to Brighton Corporation on trust, to preserve the rural nature of the village. He was succeeded as squire by Thornton-Smith who, in 1960, gave the Manor House and much of the village to the National Trust.

The Seven Sisters

BIRLING GAP, CROWLINK AND EAST DEAN

*This stunning walk begins at Birling Gap on the Sussex
Heritage Coast, from where you get a breathtaking panorama
of the Seven Sisters – a series of rolling white chalk cliffs that
stretch to Cuckmere Haven in the west – with Seaford Head
beyond. The route starts out along the South Downs Way,
following the coastline up hill and down dale over the first three
'sisters', before heading inland across the Downs towards the
charming old hamlet of Crowlink. From here you make your way
to Friston church where the graveyard is the last resting place of
many a poor soul washed ashore, and on through the meadows
towards East Dean. A short detour will take you to the historic
Tiger Inn before you head back to your starting point.*

DISTANCE:	7km (4½ miles) (circular)
TIME:	2½–3½ hours
LEVEL:	Moderate (very hilly)
START/PARKING:	Birling Gap car park, 4.5km (3 miles) west of Eastbourne (BN20 0AB). (Alternative parking available at Crowlink, starting walk midway through point 4 on the map.) OS grid reference TV554602 (OS Explorer map 123)
GETTING THERE:	*By car:* Turn off A27 from Brighton on to A26 to Newhaven, then take A259 towards Eastbourne, turning right to East Dean and continuing along road to Birling Gap *By public transport:* Take train to Brighton or Eastbourne, then catch bus no. 12 to East Dean to join walk at point 6 on the map
REFRESHMENTS:	The Tiger Inn, East Dean, or Birling Gap Café
LOCAL ATTRACTIONS:	Charleston Manor; Drusillas Park

DIRECTIONS

1. From the car park, head away from the sea and turn left on to the shingled track (behind the toilets) heading uphill. Go through the gate at the end of the track then turn left at the yellow waymark sign. Go through another gate and up on to the down. Here, cucumber-scented salad burnett, a nationally rare plant, thrives in the turf, and on warm days the air is sweet with the coconut aroma of gorse. Listen out for skylarks, rising from the grass to fill the air with their melodious song, and in the coombes (dry valleys) watch for the

dashing eye stripes and bobbing white rumps of wheatears. In summer, you will also find clouds of butterflies on the chalk grassland.

2. Follow the coastline along the South Downs Way, counting each hill as you go. From Birling Gap the Seven Sisters are Went Hill Brow, Baily's Hill, Flagstaff Brow, Brass Point, Rough Brow, Short Brow and Haven Brow, although you are only crossing the first three 'sisters' plus Flat Hill, which lies between Baily's and Flagstaff.

3. After descending the fourth hill – which has a stone memorial on top – turn right along the coombe. Before turning inland, however, take notice of the markings on the base of the hill ahead. These are the foundations of coastguard cottages, which became unsafe due to cliff erosion and were subsequently used for artillery target practice in World War II. The tranquility of this peaceful area was often shattered during the war by fighter planes thundering in from the sea to land at a nearby airfield. The unusual stone building on the hillside opposite housed the pilots. For a different kind of airborne display, visit the dew pond beside the path, where colourful dragonflies and damselflies stage spectacular summer flying shows.

CLIFFS ON THE MARCH

The Seven Sisters, along with Beachy Head to the east, mark the point where the South Downs meet the coast. First recorded in the 15th century as the Seven Cliffs, no one knows where the now more common term 'Sisters' comes from, although it actually refers to the dry valleys, or coombes, between the hills rather than to the hills themselves. The dramatic, brilliant white cliffs are the result of constant erosion of the soft chalk limestone by the action of the sea, which is eating them away at a staggering rate of 60cm (24in) per year. Extrapolating this back means that, in 1066, the cliffs would have been more than 550m (600yd) further out to sea than they are now.

4. Pass the dew pond, then bear right along the path to the gate and continue straight ahead. As you climb notice the trees to your left, sculpted by the prevailing winds to look like hunched old men. Go through Crowlink, a beautiful old hamlet centred around a manor house, and on through Crowlink car park (an alternative starting point). Carry on down the lane to the main road, then turn right through the gate into the churchyard of St Mary the Virgin, Friston. Look out here for the simple graves of unknown people who were 'washed ashore' – some date back to 1830.

5. Go through the far gate and follow the path down through the meadow. This lovely hay meadow is known as Hobbs Eares. In Sussex dialect 'eares' means arable land, and Hobbs would have been the surname of the owner. In spring the meadow is a sea of white and yellow daisies and buttercups; in summer a wave of deep purple and gold washes over it as knapweed appears through the drying grass.

6. Near the bottom of the meadow, veer right and pick up the path through the trees. (Alternatively, if you are in need of refreshment, the gate at the bottom of Hobbs Eares takes you to East Dean village and the historic Tiger Inn – just bear right on to the road and follow it to the green then turn left.) At the top, bear right and climb the hill, heading towards the steps set in the wall to your left. Watch where you tread in early spring: the hillside is a site for the rare early spider orchid, the flowers of which looking every bit like black furry bodies. Go over the steps and head uphill towards the gate. If you hear a loud laughing call from the trees to your left, you have probably disturbed a green woodpecker. It has brilliant green and yellow feathers and a red crown – but all you are likely to see is its yellow rump as it swoops away from you.

7. Cross the stile beside the gate and skirt round the left of the field. Go through the kissing gate and cross the field towards the red barn. As you approach the barn, bear right to pick up the well-defined sunken track. Follow this over the hill and keep straight ahead towards the sea, passing through two gates until you reach the gate you passed through on your outward journey. Turn left through this gate and on to the track leading back to Birling Gap and your starting point.

Courtesy of The National Trust. For more information go to www.nationaltrust.org.uk or telephone 01243 814554 for a copy of 'Stroll the South Downs' walks pack.

Heritage Coastline Walk

EAST DEAN, BIRLING GAP AND BEACHY HEAD

*This glorious walk takes you along part of the
Sussex Heritage Coast, one of Britain's most spectacular
coastlines with its rich wildlife and high chalk cliffs, marking the
point where the South Downs plunge into the sea. Setting off the
from village of East Dean, the walk takes you across the most
easterly of the Seven Sisters (a series of rolling cliffs) and on to
Birling Gap, which provides the only access to the sea for several
miles. From here you follow the South Downs Way to the Belle
Tout Lighthouse, beyond which you are rewarded with
outstanding views over Beachy Head before heading inland
for the return journey through fields and country lanes.*

DISTANCE:	5.5km (3½ miles) (circular)
TIME:	Allow 1½–2 hours
LEVEL:	Moderate (with some steep climbs)
START/PARKING:	East Dean car park off Gilberts Drive (nearby post code BN20 0DA). OS grid reference TV557778 (OS Explorer map 123)
GETTING THERE:	*By car:* Turn off A27 from Brighton on to A26 to Newhaven, then take A259 towards Eastbourne, turning right to East Dean *By public transport:* Take train to Eastbourne then catch bus no. 12 to East Dean
REFRESHMENTS:	The Tiger Inn
LOCAL ATTRACTIONS:	Seven Sisters Sheep Centre

DIRECTIONS

1. From the car park, turn right towards the village green and then left opposite The Tiger Inn, passing the war memorial on your right. At the far corner of the green, bear left on to Went Way (the upper of two roads). This is the oldest road in the district, along which Neolithic men, Saxons, Romans, pedlars, mariners and smugglers have all passed. Continue along the road until you reach the five-barred gate.

2. Pass through the gate and you are immediately on the first of the Seven Sisters, known as Went Hill. Take the upward pathway straight ahead through another gate and climb through a steep wooded area to a seat on your right. Here you may be lucky enough to hear the yaffle (laughing call) of a green woodpecker and, in springtime, the call of the cuckoo. From here you have a splendid view to the south of Birling Manor nestling in the valley and, beyond the landmark of an old lighthouse known as Belle Tout, your first glimpse of the sea.

3. Continue uphill, then bear left at the top (where the path peters out), heading towards a red barn. As you approach the barn bear right to join up with a well-defined sunken track that takes you down towards the sea and open downland. This area is rich in wildlife – look out for skylarks, meadow pipits, pied wagtails, fieldfares, kestrels and peregrine falcons, to name but a few of the birds, and bird's-foot trefoil, buttercup, bee orchid, purple orchid, scabious, and viper's bugloss among the many flower species.

4. Leave the main path where it bends left and go through the gate, heading straight towards the sea. Pass through another gate and carry straight on down the path through scrubby gorse and blackberry brambles. Shortly after, turn sharp left through a gateway on to a shingled road between bungalows, and walk parallel to the coastline until you meet the main road at Birling Gap. Turn right for refreshments and the beach.

5. The Gap provides the only access to the sea between Eastbourne and Cuckmere Haven, and in the past was associated with smuggling, chiefly of spirits such as Geneva (gin) and brandy. Turn your back to the beach and pass the row of old coastguard cottages. By the telephone kiosk (if it's still there!) and coastguard's office turn sharp right and climb the hill to the coastguard lookout at the top of the cliff. From here, if you turn back to face the Gap, you get a magnificent view of the Seven Sisters.

6. Continue along the footpath as it climbs towards Belle Tout, a lighthouse built in 1834 and financed by 'Mad Jack' Fuller of Brightling, better known for building follies. The lighthouse was put out of service in 1903 when the modern Beachy Head lighthouse was built, and in 1999 it was moved in its entirety in to avoid it collapsing into the sea along with the eroding cliff face.

7. Follow the footpath round the back of the lighthouse and carry on towards the road, pausing to admire Beachy Head – at 162m (530ft) the highest chalk sea cliff in Britain – and the lighthouse ahead of you. Just before the road, turn left to follow the path leading back towards Birling Gap (there may be a gate and electric fence here). As you walk, keep a look out on your right for a five-barred gate and a concrete track on the opposite side of the road.

8. Turn right towards the gate, crossing the road and passing through the gap beside the gate: you are now standing on what was once a Roman road. Follow the track until you reach the top of the hill, where the track bears right towards Cornish Farm. Carry straight on here, across the grass and through two footpath gates. Remain on the footpath and you soon come to a low flint wall built by Napoleonic prisoners-of-war in 1793. Continue to follow the path until you reach the edge of Birling Manor, probably built during the reign of Henry VII and subsequently added to and altered by successive yeoman farmers. Go through two bridle gates and follow the gravel drive to the road leading to Birling Gap.

9. On your right is the Seven Sisters Sheep Centre, which has one of the largest collections of sheep in the world, with over 40 breeds. Walk straight ahead along the road towards East Dean village until you reach the small gate under a brick arch on your left. Take the path leading to the East Dean parish church of St Simon and St Jude. The oldest part of this church is the Saxon tower, dating back to before the Norman Conquest.

10. Leave the churchyard by the tapsel gate – these swing gates are peculiar to Sussex, made by one John Tapsel – and walk up the short hill back to the village green and on to your starting point.

Courtesy of the residents of East Dean and the Gilbert Estate.
For more information go to wwww.beachyhead.org.uk

The Drovers Circuit

SINGLETON, DROVERS ESTATE AND CHARLTON

*Beginning in the pretty village of Singleton, just
north of the Goodwood Racecourse, this attractive walk takes
you across the Drovers, a traditional countryside estate with
rolling hills, woods and farmland managed by the National Trust.
Drovers has long been connected with country sports: pheasant
shooting still takes place from September to late January (usually
Saturdays) and you may be asked to wait briefly while a drive is
completed. Highlights of the route include Nightingale Wood,
which is aflame with oranges, reds and yellows in autumn,
and Levin Down, where, in the summer, a wealth of flowers
and butterflies add a blaze of colour and the buzz of
grasshoppers and the scent of wild thyme fill the air.*

DISTANCE:	6.5km (4 miles) (circular)
TIME:	Allow 2–3 hours
LEVEL:	Strenuous (with steep climbs, numerous stiles and muddy tracks)
START/PARKING:	Cricket pitch in Singleton (PO18 0HA). On-street parking at Singleton or Weald and Downland Museum. OS grid reference SU874130 (OS Explorer map 120)
GETTING THERE:	*By car:* Turn off A286 Chichester/Midhurst road 8km (5 miles) north of Chichester *By public transport:* Train to Chichester, then bus no. 60 towards Midhurst
REFRESHMENTS:	The Fox Goes Free, Charlton, or The Partridge Inn, Singleton
LOCAL ATTRACTIONS:	Weald and Downland Open Air Museum, Singleton; West Dean Gardens

DIRECTIONS

1. From the cricket pitch, walk along the A286 towards the village, then turn left on to a footpath that takes you over a bridge and around the cricket pavilion. Cross three stiles and continue uphill along the sunken track. The hedgerow along this track is a weave of hawthorn, ash, hazel, oak and dogwood. The wealth of species indicates that it is very old.

2. Cross the bridge over the disused railway, once part of the Chichester to Midhurst line but closed to passengers in 1935. After crossing the bridge, go sharp right up to the stile. Cross the stile and bear left at the fingerpost up Hat

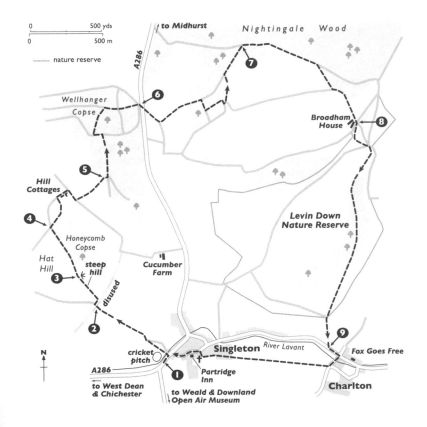

Hill. In summer, the hillside is speckled with the yellow, blue and pink of cowslips, harebells and common spotted orchids, and the air is scented with wild thyme.

3. Before reaching the brow of the hill, pause to look back at the views. In the valley to your left is Cucumber Farm which dates back to the 1700s. The name is thought to derive from 'cow-combe', relating to the farm's use for dairy farming. On the horizon to the right you can see the gleaming white stands of Goodwood Racecourse. Follow the path through the wood. Here, in the dappled shade of Honeycomb Copse, you will find many ancient, gnarled beech trees, some planted in the 1800s to commemorate the Battle of Trafalgar.

4. When you emerge, cross the open grassy area, go over the stile, and carry straight on round the field edge to the next gate. This area was once the centre of an extensive deer park, recorded as being owned by the Earl of Arundel in 1327. Turn right and walk past Hill Cottages, then go right again. At the hedge, veer off to the left and follow the path across the arable field.

5. At the far side, go over the stile into Wellhanger Copse. At the junction, turn left and follow the path to the next junction. Go left, then next right up the path. Look out for the coppiced hazel trees here. Coppicing is the traditional practice of cutting stems back to stumps, so that numerous new shoots grow. These shoots are used for making fencing and thatching spars. At the next junction go right, then straight over the crossroads and down to the main road.

6. Cross the road with care and follow the track opposite. After about 100m (100yd) take the first track to the left which takes you around a field to Nightingale Wood. In the wood, take the first track off to the right and after about 70m (70yd), at the top of a steep rise, go left. At the next junction, turn right and follow the path to the next junction. Turn left and walk to the top of the hill, then stay on the main path as it goes through the beech wood. As you walk down this path in April, you will be greeted by a stunning cascade of bluebells on the other side of the valley.

7. At the T-junction, turn right and follow the track round, up the steep hill and down the other side, following the edge of the wood. As you descend, look out

LEVIN DOWN

A Site of Special Scientific Interest, Levin Down stands out against the surrounding landscape as a lone hill covered in natural scrubby grassland. Its name hints at the reason why the wildlife here is so rich, 'Levin' being derived from 'leave-alone hill', reflecting the fact that the hillsides are too steep for the plough or other intensive agriculture. In summer, an abundance of butterflies can be found, such as the brown argus, brown hairstreak, blues, dingy and grizzled skippers, and the rare Duke of Burgundy, while chalk grassland flowers include clustered bellflower, chalk heath, juniper, milkwort, fairy flax, wild thyme and pyramid orchid.

for the spiny evergreen shrub, butcher's broom, amidst the holly. In the past, this plant was used by butchers to clean their chopping blocks – feel it and you'll know why. Follow the path down through the meadows.

8. Go through the farm gates at Broadham House and take the steep path to the right. Climb up through the field, through a small gate at the top, then turn right and go through another gate. Bear left up the hill, walking alongside the wood. Halfway up, go over the stile beside the gate into the wood and follow the narrow path, crossing over the next stile. You are now in Levin Down Nature Reserve, owned by the Goodwood Estate and leased to the Sussex Wildlife Trust. Keep on the path, following it downhill over several stiles then across the field on to the road.

9. Turn left along the road towards Charlton, then right at the crossroads. After about 100m (110yd) turn right on to the footpath and follow it across the arable field (or turn left to visit The Fox Goes Free first). At the far side, follow the path to the right, cross the road and continue past the church and through the gate, then turn right on to the lane. Go left at the road, and left again on to the main road to take you back to your starting point.

Courtesy of The National Trust. For more information go to www.nationaltrust.org.uk

Black Down Woodland Walk

*With its wild beauty and multiple viewpoints,
affording views of the English Channel on a clear day, this
delightful walk takes you through one of Britain's most rapidly
disappearing habitats – lowland heathland. Sited in the Weald,
but forming part of the South Downs National Park, Black
Down is the highest point in West Sussex at 280m (919ft) and
is managed by the National Trust, which is working to restore
the open heathland (see special feature). Part of the main
walk lies across an uneven and hilly terrain, with one steep
climb, but an optional shortcut allows walkers to remain
on even ground for the duration of the route.*

DISTANCE:	5km (3¼ miles) (circular) or shorter, more even route of 4.5km (3 miles)
TIME:	Allow 1½ – 2 hours
LEVEL:	Moderate (with one steep climb) or easy shorter route
START/PARKING:	Car park in Tennyson's Lane, Haslemere (nearby post code GU27 3AF). OS grid reference SU920308 (OS Explorer map 133)
GETTING THERE:	*By car:* Take A286 to Haslemere and turn off on to B2131 Petworth road; take second right on to Haste Hill, then turn right on to Tennyson's Lane (signposted to Black Down) *By public transport:* Train to Haslemere Station, then walk to starting point (about 40 minutes)
REFRESHMENTS:	A selection of pubs and cafés in Haslemere
LOCAL ATTRACTIONS:	Haslemere Museum

DIRECTIONS

1. From the car park, go up the track that leads off the lane, past the second car park and continue straight ahead, passing the interpretation board. After about 200m (220yd), a track – the Sussex Border Path – joins from the left. Continue on up the sunken lane edged with bilberry and gorse, surrounded by coniferous and mixed woodland.

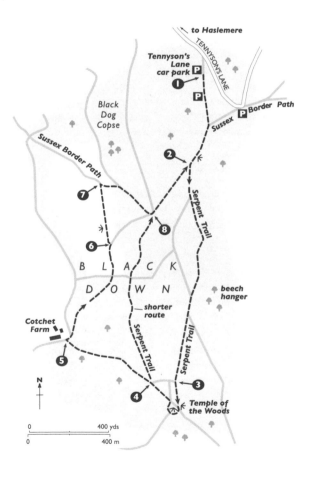

2. Turn left after a short distance to the viewpoint and seat for good views to the south-east. Return to the main track and continue along it for about 75m (82yd) until you reach a fork. Turn left here and follow the Serpent Trail, bearing left again at the next fork. Carry on along the track, ignoring any side paths, and pass through the beech hanger (steeply wooded hillside). Continue straight ahead at the junction and bear right at the fork on the Serpent Trail.

3. At the next main fork, bear left on the National Trust path down through the staggered gates to the spectacular viewpoint. Here you will find an orientation board and a stone seat commemorating Edward Hunter's wife. Follow the path on and through the staggered gates. Continue along the path, bearing right to the main track and the fingerpost. Turn left on the Serpent Trail.

4. At the next junction, you have a choice of route. For those wishing a shorter, more level walk, continue on the main track, bearing slightly right. Follow this path until you join up with the longer route (go to direction 8, below). To continue with the longer, more hilly walk, go straight ahead along the sandy stony track leading downhill. Continue down through a grassy valley to the National Trust board and Cotchet Farm.

5. Turn right up the lane, bearing round past the house with the outbuildings on your left. Fork right uphill, off the main track, on a steep and often muddy bridleway. Carry on through the holly and rhododendron glade, watered by the many springs that rise in this area, noting the abundant moss along the way. Continue as the path opens out into heathland with gorse.

6. Almost at the top of the rise, bear sharply left on a new National Trust path with views to the south and south-west. Follow the path as it winds through the area recently cleared of trees to restore the heathland, turning left to reach the viewpoint and seat, from where you can admire the wonderful views. Return to the main path and continue along it until you reach the junction with the Sussex Border Path.

7. Turn right along the Sussex Border Path, passing small hollows on either side where chert was quarried. A type of hard sandstone mined by the local community, chert was used throughout the area for building boundary banks, roads and buildings. From here, to your left, you get wonderful views to the Hog's Back (a chalk ridge running between Guildford and Farnham) and Gibbet Hill, Hindhead, the second highest point in Surrey, where the corpses of highwaymen were once displayed to deter others from following in their footsteps.

8. At the junction of the five paths, where the alternative route joins from the right, bear left along the main track. (On the alternative route continue straight ahead here.) Follow the track, ignoring any side paths and passing the boggy area and peat ponds on your left. Here you may see dragonflies and damselflies. Stay on the main path until you join the track you came along from the car park, near the first viewpoint. Retrace your steps along this path to return to Tennyson's Lane car park, ignoring the right-hand fork along the Sussex Border Path.

Courtesy of Haslemere Visitor and Local Information Centre and the National Trust. For more information go to www.haslemere.com/vic and www.nationaltrust.org.uk

RESTORING THE HEATHLAND

Heathlands were created thousands of years ago by early humans, who cleared the forests in order to graze their animals. Without fertilizers this practice constantly 'stripped' the soil of nutrients so that nothing but hardy heathers and grasses would grow. Black Down has changed dramatically over the past 60 years as the people who once used the land have died out. In the absence of grazing, invasive trees and plants quickly overtook the heathers, shading them from sunlight and threatening the wildlife that depended on the heath for its survival. In order to restore the heathland and conserve the precious wildlife associated with it, the National Trust undertakes selected felling of trees and has reintroduced grazing in the area.

Ancient Tracks and Forts

FULKING DOWNS

*Perched on the northern escarpment of the South Downs,
just north of Brighton, this exhilarating walk across National
Trust land takes you through some spectacular scenery, with views
reaching as far as London on a clear day. The number 77 bus, part
of a special bus service called 'Breeze up to the Downs', takes you
to your starting point, making it easier than ever to leave the
car at home. From here you head steeply down the scarp towards
the village of Fulking, then skirt around the foot of the hillside
before climbing back to the top of the downs, following ancient
sheep tracks and passing a Victorian lime kiln and an
Iron Age hill fort along the way.*

DISTANCE: **5.5km (3½ miles) (circular)**
TIME: **Allow 1½–2½ hours**
LEVEL: **Moderate (with one steep climb)**

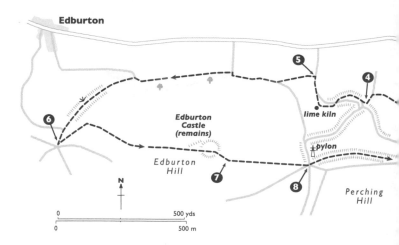

START/PARKING: **The Devil's Dyke pub, 9.5km (6 miles) north of Hove (BN1 8YJ). Park in National Trust car park (fees apply). OS grid reference TQ258110 (OS Explorer map 122)**

GETTING THERE: *By car:* Turn north off A27 at Hove on to Devil's Dyke Road, following signs for Devil's Dyke
By public transport: Train to Brighton then take bus no. 77 to Devil's Dyke (show rail tickets for 2-for-1 offer)

REFRESHMENTS: **The Devil's Dyke public house or The Shepherd and Dog in Fulking**

LOCAL ATTRACTIONS: **Royal Pavilion, Brighton**

DIRECTIONS

1. Before you leave the crowds behind, get your bearings by looking at the viewpoint by the stone seat. Fulking Hill – your destination – is to your left as you look out over the scarp slope. Follow the path to the left (opposite the pub), going through the kissing gate and heading straight on towards the cleft in the grassy bank. These grassy mounds form the ramparts of an Iron Age hill fort. If the fort was under attack, sheep and cattle may have been herded inside for safekeeping.

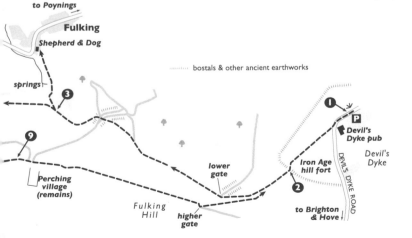

2. After passing through the bank, walk along the ridge, making for the signpost to the lower of the two bridle gates up ahead. Go through gate and down the main track to the right. En route,

you will suddenly come across deep hollows, known as bostals, which date back to Medieval times. These are tracks etched into the chalk by sheep being driven daily from their night-time pens in fallow fields on to the downs. Notice the 'dual carriage-way' where two bostals run side by side. Continue along the path until you reach a fork in the track by a National Trust sign.

3. Bear left at the fork. Alternatively, take a short detour down the path to the right to see the spring at The Shepherd and Dog pub in Fulking. The spring is one of three that gush from this stretch of the downs – the villages of Fulking, Edburton and Poynings have developed around them. To continue your walk, carry on following the main track, forking left at the junction and crossing the stile. After going through a hollow, go left up a path. Cross the stile then turn right and take the steps into the bostal.

4. Follow the track down, taking the left-hand bostal at the fork. Near the bottom of the bostal, look left to see a wall with a hole in the base. This is a

PROTECTING THE LANDSCAPE

Sheep have been a constant feature on Fulking Downs for 4,000 years: their grazing has resulted in the wildlife-rich grassland we see today. Without sheep grazing, thorny bushes would quickly invade the grassland and shade out the wildlife.

The National Trust, which owns large areas of land along this stretch of the South Downs escarpment, is continuing the grazing tradition and removing any bushes that have taken hold in order to protect the wildlife and restore the ancient landscape. Orchids are common here, as are chalkland butterflies, including several species of blue. A number of rare species of grasshopper can also be found.

Victorian lime kiln, recently restored by the National Trust: the information panel will tell you more about it.

5. Turn left before the five-barred gate and follow the path over two stiles. Skirt the foot of the hill until you reach a waymark post. Take the left fork and follow the bostal uphill. Halfway up the hill, take a well-earned rest to view the panorama. You can clearly see the three spring-line villages: Edburton in front of you, Fulking to the right and Poynings beyond.

6. Before reaching the gate at top of the hill, turn left and follow the fence-line along the ridge. The curious mounds you cross are the Medieval remains of Edburton Castle, thought to have been a look-out post for nearby Bramber Castle. Cross the mounds and go through the right-hand stile.

7. Walk gently downhill towards the pylon on the edge of the ridge. Over the past 50 years, 90 per cent of chalk grassland in Britain has been ploughed up. The field you are crossing met a similar fate until coming under the care of the Trust in 1987. It has since been restored to grass. In time, flowers such as cowslips, orchids and wild thyme will reappear.

8. Go through the wooden gate and take the narrow path that goes uphill (to the left of the main track). Along the way, take a closer look at the sides of the bostal. On your left is the sunny south-facing slope, sprinkled with grassland flowers. In June, wild thyme steals the show with its mauve flowers and delicate scent. The damper, north-facing slope supports bright green mosses, which enliven the weary winter grassland.

9. Go through the next gate and along the ridge track. On the right is the site of the deserted Medieval village of Perching. People moved here in the 13th century when over-population forced them to the less-hospitable downs. You can still make out the ancient terraces formed by ploughing. The village was probably abandoned after the Black Death (bubonic plague) had wiped out much of Britain's population. Once again, the downs became the exclusive domain of sheep. Over the brow, head towards the higher gate, then follow the path back to your starting point at The Devil's Dyke pub.

Courtesy of The National Trust. For more information go to www.nationaltrust.org.uk or telephone 01243 814554 for a copy of 'Stroll the South Downs' walks pack.

Harting Down Wildlife Walk

*This short walk across Harting Down in West
Sussex affords spectacular panoramic views of the
surrounding countryside and a rich array of wildlife. Rising
to 229m (751ft), the site is one of the largest areas of ancient
chalk downland in National Trust care, and is a renowned nature
reserve and Site of Special Scientific Interest. Along the way you
will encounter a wealth of wild flowers and butterflies, and
be serenaded by skylarks and nightingales. There are also
earthworks and an Iron Age hill fort to explore, and
a recently excavated dew pond that teems
with insect life and amphibians.*

DISTANCE:	3km (2 miles) (circular) with 3km (2 miles) extension starting from South Harting
TIME:	Allow 1–1½ hours (with extension: 2–2½ hours)
LEVEL:	Moderate (with steep climbs and descents)
START/PARKING:	National Trust car park (free to members); alternative parking in South Harting, south of church on B2141, with 1.5km (1 mile) walk to starting point (nearby post code: GU31 5QB). OS grid reference SU791180 (OS Explorer map 120)
GETTING THERE:	*By car:* Take A3 to Petersfield, turning off on to A272 Midhurst road; then take B2199, merging into the B2146 to South Harting, turning off on to B2141 to Harting Down
	By public transport: Train to Petersfield, then take bus no. 54 towards Chichester or no. 91 towards Midhurst, alighting in South Harting and walking 1.5km (1 mile) to starting point
REFRESHMENTS:	The White Hart Inn, South Harting
LOCAL ATTRACTIONS:	Uppark House and Gardens

DIRECTIONS

1. Starting in Harting Down National Trust car park, walk through the gate and follow the path across Harting Hill. Alternatively, if you parked in South Harting, follow the footpath up through the hangers (steeply wooded hillside) until you reach the South Downs Way. Turn left here, crossing the road (B2146) with care and following the path until you reach another road (B2141). Cross the road to join up with the path that takes you across Harting Down. Harting Down has traditionally been grazed by sheep, a practice the National Trust maintains in order to conserve the rich grassland environment with its wealth of wildlife (see special feature, page 91).

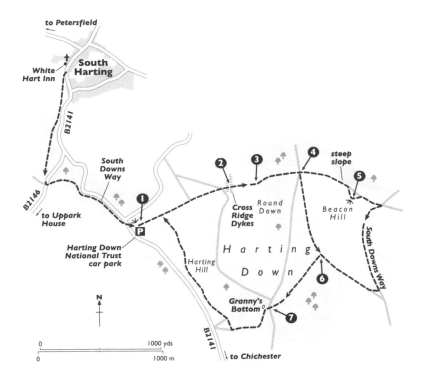

2. Go over the undulating earthworks, or Cross Ridge Dykes. These parallel mounds probably had fences on top and date back to the Iron Age, when they may have served as boundary markers or a 'checkpoint' controlling the movement of people and animals across the ridgeway. Follow the right-hand track up Round Down hill, keeping a hedge on your left. You'll see a huge variety of plants here all year round.

3. Just over the top of the hill turn left and go through a gate, before walking down into the next valley. Pass through another gate at the bottom and walk across to the base of Beacon Hill – the site of an Iron Age hill fort that was probably created as an animal enclosure and symbol of status, rather than a defensive stronghold. Here you can catch a whiff of the berries that grow on the female juniper bush and, in springtime, enjoy a buttery-yellow carpet of cowslips, often used to make potent local wine.

4. At the junction you can choose either to follow the path straight ahead and ascend Beacon Hill or turn right and skirt around the hill's lower slopes, avoiding the steep climb. The latter route follows the South Downs Way to point 6 on the map, where you turn right (go straight to direction 6, below). If you take the route over the top, climb steeply uphill then bear right off the main path to reach the summit, where you will find some concrete foundations. These are the only remains of a 'shutter' telegraph station, one of a series built in the late 18th century to warn of a French invasion. Shutters on the roof of the station would be opened and closed in sequence to send coded messages from Portsmouth (on this route) to the Admiralty in London, a process that took only 15 minutes. After 1814, the shutter system was replaced by semaphore telegraphy.

5. From the top, follow the path downhill to a crossroads of paths and turn sharp right on to another section of the South Downs Way. Skirt back round the lower slopes of Beacon Hill, turning sharp right among the trees and continuing along the path until you come to a junction where you meet up with the shorter route at point 6, on the map.

6. At the signpost turn left away from Beacon Hill (right if you took the short-cut down from point 4 on the map) and follow the path down to a dew pond and a little hill, known as Granny's Bottom, on your right. The dew pond in the valley bottom was re-created in the 1990s on the site of a 17th-century pond. There are several such man-made ponds on Harting Down, which collect rainwater rather than dew and were originally used to supply water to grazing animals. The ponds are no longer needed for sheep but are rich in wildlife, such as frogs and dragonflies.

7. Pass the pond and cross into a yew wood, known as 'the darkest place on the downs': it is cold in here, even on a hot day. Yew trees are home to birds such as wrens, thrushes and finches. Climb up through the shade, turning right to follow the path back on to Harting Hill. You finally emerge from the wood through an opening (not a gate) on the right. Stay on the grassy path back to the car park, or retrace your steps back to South Harting.

Courtesy of The National Trust. For more information go to www.nationaltrust.org.uk or telephone 01243 814554 for a copy of 'Stroll the South Downs' walks pack.

WILDLIFE WATCH

The grasslands on Harting Down support a wealth of plant species such as cowslips, chalk milkwort, bird's-foot trefoil and musk, pyramidal and fragrant orchids. The area is also one of the best places in Britain for juniper, whose fragrant black berries are used in gin-making. The small hummocky mounds strewn across the hillsides are the nests of the yellow meadow ant, which retain heat from the sun to keep the colonies warm. Strangely, the ants help care for the caterpillars of the common blue butterfly, in return for a sugary secretion that they produce. Other invertebrates include the Duke of Burgundy fritillary and the grizzled skipper butterflies, the blue carpenter bee and the rare cheese snail. Look out for fallow deer grazing in the evening light near 'Granny's Bottom', and listen out for nightingales on summer afternoons and evenings. If you are really lucky, you may even catch the rare sight of male adders 'dancing' (wrestling) for territory.

Useful Contacts

Angmering Parish Council
The Corner House
The Square
Angmering
West Sussex
BN16 4EA
tel: 01903 850756
email: admin@angmering-pc.gov.uk;
www.angmeringparishcouncil.gov.uk

Beachyhead
The Gilbert Estate Office
Upper Street
East Dean
East Sussex
BN20 0BY
email: info@beachyhead.org.uk
www.beachyhead.org.uk

Footprints of Sussex
Pear Tree Cottage
Jarvis Lane
Steyning
BN44 3GL
tel: 01903 813381
email: info@footprintsofsussex.co.uk
www.footprintsofsussex.co.uk
*(walking holidays and local
guided walks)*

The Countryside Agency
tel: 01242 521381
www.countryside.gov.uk
*(For more details regarding public rights
of way see: Out in the Country – Where
you can go and what you can do)*

**Haslemere Visitor and Local
Information Centre**
Haslemere Educational Museum
78 High Street
Haslemere
Surrey
GU27 2LA
tel: 01428 645425
email: vic@haslemere.com
www.haslemere.com/vic

Per-Rambulations
Larkshill
Cranston Road
East Grinstead
West Sussex
RH19 3HL
tel: 01342 315786
email: info@per-rambulations.co.uk
www.per-rambulations.co.uk
*(guided walks and publisher of local
walking guides)*

Seven Sisters Country Park
Exceat
Seaford
East Sussex
BN25 4AD
tel: 01323 870280
email: sevensisters@south
downs-aonb.gov.uk
www.sevensisters.org.uk

**South Downs National
Park Authority**
Rosemary's Parlour
North Street
Midhurst
West Sussex
GU29 9SB
tel: 0300 303 1053
email: info@southdowns.gov.uk
www.southdowns.gov.uk

South Downs Society
2 Swan Court
Station Road
Pulborough
RH20 1RL
tel: 01798 875073
email: info@southdownssociety.org.uk
www.southdownssociety.org.uk

South Downs Way National Trail
Victorian Barn
Victorian Business Centre
Ford Road, Ford
West Sussex
BN18 0EF
tel: 01243 558716
email: sdw@southdowns-aonb.gov.uk
www.nationaltrail.co.uk/southdowns

Steyning Parish Council
email: see online contact form
www.steyningsouthdowns.com

Visit Sussex
tel: 01243 263065 or 01243 379819
email: info@visitsussex.org or use
online contact form
www.visitsussex.org

Walberton Action Group
www.walbertonag.org.uk

WILDLIFE

Hampshire and Isle of Wight Wildlife Trust
Northern Office
The Old Cartshed
Herriard Park
Basingstoke
Hampshire
RG25 2PL
tel: 01256 381190 or 01256 381186
email: feedback@hwt.org.uk
www.hwt.org.uk

RSPB (Royal Society for the Protection of Birds)
www.rspb.org.uk.
(As this is a charity, to save time and money, please try to answer queries using the online search facility before emailing via online contact form; if urgent, call 01767 693680 for membership enquiries or 01767 693690 for bird and wildlife advice.)

Sussex Wildlife Trust
Woods Mill
Henfield
West Sussex
BN5 9SD
tel: 01273 492630
email: see online contact form
www.sussexwt.org.uk

WWT (Wildfowl and Wetlands Trust)
Slimbridge
Gloucestershire
GL2 7BT
tel: 01453 891900 (press 9 for a list of options)
email: enquiries@wwt.org.uk
www.wwt.org.uk

HERITAGE ORGANIZATIONS

English Heritage
Regional Office
Eastgate Court
195–205 High Street
Guildford
GU1 3EH
tel: 0870 333 1181
email: see online contact form
www.english-heritage.org.uk

The National Trust
PO Box 39
Warrington
WA5 7WD
tel: 0844 800 1895
email: enquiries@nationaltrust.org.uk
www.nationaltrust.org.uk

Natural England
East and West Sussex Office
Phoenix House
33 North Street
Lewes
East Sussex
BN7 2PH
tel: 0300 060 0300
email: gloucestershire@natural
england.org.uk
www.naturalengland.org.uk

TRAVEL ADVICE

By car: go to the AA's Route Planner at
www.theaa.com, under 'Travel and Leisure'.

By bus: go to Traveline at www.traveline.org.uk
(0871 200 2233) or Travel Search at www.carlberry.co.uk
See also www.brighton-hove.gov.uk and search for
'Breeze up to the Downs' for bus timetables to local
countryside attractions.

By train: go to National Rail Enquiries at
www.nationalrail.co.uk (08457 48 49 50).